Y027929

LONDON or ewed
MURDERS

D1637896

LONDON MURDERS

In the Footsteps of the Capital's Killers

DAVID LONG

David Long has been a writer and journalist for more than thirty years. He has regularly appeared in *The Times*, *Sunday Times* and *Evening Standard*, and writes for children as well as adults. Well received by reviewers and readers alike, his previous titles on the capital include *London's 100 Strangest Places*, *London's 100 Most Extraordinary Buildings*, *London Underground* and *The Little Book of London* (all The History Press). His books have been translated into more than twenty languages.

First published 2020

The History Press
97 St George's Place, Cheltenham,
Gloucestershire, GL50 3QB
www.thehistorypress.co.uk

British Library Cataloguing in Publication Data.
A catalogue record for this book is available from the British Library.

ISBN 978 0 7509 9505 4

Typesetting and origination by The History Press
Printed and bound in Great Britain by TJ International Ltd.

CONTENTS

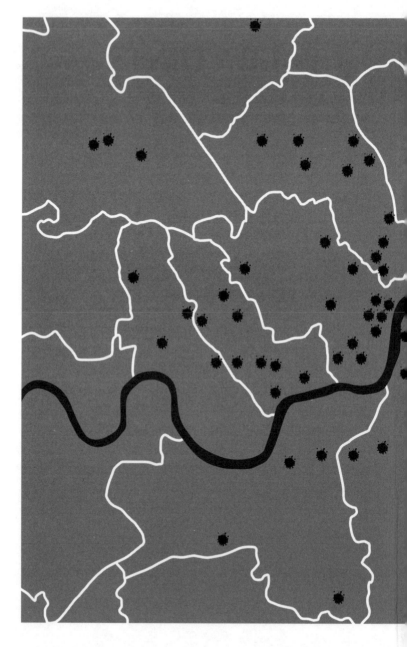

INTRODUCTION

People love a good murder. Graphically violent television dramas about killers have replaced public executions as popular entertainment, and the increasingly sophisticated science of forensics has gone a long way towards usurping traditional, old-fashioned sleuthing and inspired guesswork. But there is nothing new about our fascination with murderers – in the past racehorses, greyhounds and even a ship have been named after the most notorious – nor is there any sign that this is diminishing.

From the Ripper to Ronnie and Reggie Kray, we can always be relied upon to find the specific details shocking, and the fact that the victim is a complete stranger rarely does much to reduce our feelings of revulsion, fear or horror. There is also a definite, if macabre, thrill to be had from following the slow-motion unravelling of discovery, detection, confession and conviction – and a genuine frisson of excitement on passing an address made famous by its grisly past.

Murders happen all the time, of course, and only a minority of them have that special attribute needed to command our attention. When that happens, the media is skilled at playing its part in whipping up public interest and crime reporters have a long history of rearranging the facts where necessary in order to construct a more compelling narrative. As long ago as 1847, for example, several newspapers famously ran breathless accounts of the dignified courtroom composure of murderess Mary Ann Milner – despite her having been found hanging in her cell the previous day.

Even without this kind of encouragement, however, the urge to glimpse a killer in the flesh and see justice done has always been strong, and around this same time a German visitor planning a trip to London was told in all seriousness, 'You wish to know where the people's merry-makings are held? Go to Newgate on a hanging day ... there you will find shouting, and joking, and junketting, from early dawn until the hangman has made his appearance and performed his office.'

On such occasions, great stands would be erected for spectators, and landlords of taverns fortunate enough to occupy sites overlooking the scaffold would charge a premium for their beer and brandy – well in excess of what Londoners would have stood for on an ordinary weekday – and spectators of both sexes, every age and literally all classes would have thronged the streets in the hope of witnessing an actual execution.

Today, we like to think we are more civilised than this, yet the attraction – enjoyment might not be too strong a word for it – has never really gone away. The decision to abandon public hangings was deeply unpopular; so too was the abolition of capital punishment in the 1960s, and lifelike waxworks of serial killers and other murderers have always numbered among Madame Tussaud's most popular attractions.

Indeed, even now, many decades after their conviction and imprisonment or execution, London's worst murderers find themselves as celebrated as any of the city's more talented or public-spirited inhabitants. Names such as Crippen, Christie and Ellis are woven into the fabric of London's cultural history alongside those of Whittington, Wren and Disraeli. Similarly, while most visitors to the capital still seek out the likes of St Paul's, the Tower and Westminster Abbey, many others pore over books and maps looking to pinpoint such infamous addresses as 10 Rillington Place, 39 Hilldrop Crescent or Whitechapel's notorious Blind Beggar.

1

EAST OF
THE CITY

JOHN WILLIAMS

29 The Highway, E1 (1811)
Cannon Street Road/Cable Street crossroads, E1
(1811)
Cinnamon Street, E1 (1811)

The Ratcliffe Highway Murders

For years, convicted murderers were buried without ceremony beneath the prisons at which they died, and a total of 119 bodies – including those of Crippen and Christie – are believed to lie beneath the gardens at Pentonville, dating back to when London's own Death Row moved there from Newgate in 1902. Occasionally, particular convicts are singled out for special treatment, although very rarely with the gruesome glee that seems to have attended the occasion in 1811 when the remains of John Williams were consigned to an especially bleak spot in East London.

Williams was widely believed to be the perpetrator of a series of bloody killings which came to be called the Ratcliffe Highway Murders. The first was committed at what is now No. 29 The Highway. The building itself is long gone, although a wealth of old warehouses and wharf buildings in the area still give some indication of how this area adjacent to the docks might have looked in the early nineteenth century.

In 1811, No. 29 was a hosiery business, the owner of which, 24-year-old Timothy Marr, lived on the premises with his wife and child. On the evening of 7 December, he asked the servant girl Margaret to go out for some oysters and on her return, she found the family dead. Together with an apprentice from the shop, all of them had had their throats cut and their heads staved in using a bloody ship's hammer, or maul, which was recovered at the scene.

To avoid panic in the tight knot of the surrounding streets, the authorities quickly rustled up the offer of a £500 reward for the murderer's capture – this at a time when the Governor of the Bank of England received just £400 annually. It was generous, but to no avail.

Exactly two weeks later at the King's Arms Tavern, in what is now Glamis Road, the landlord John Williamson was similarly done to death, together with his wife, Elizabeth, and Bridget Harrington, who helped behind the bar. On this occasion, there was a witness – a lodger who managed to escape from a back bedroom by climbing down a sheet he had knotted to the window.

With the public clamouring for some affirmative action, the authorities were soon able to announce a number of arrests, though one of them – a seaman called John Williams, who was apprehended on 21 December in Cinnamon Street – aroused no particular interest. He had been seen drinking in the King's Arms, and after being interviewed by magistrates at Shadwell, he was remanded in custody at Cold Bath Fields Prison in Clerkenwell. (The site is now occupied by the giant Mount Pleasant Sorting Office.)

The evidence against Williams was, to say the least, extremely slim, and 200 years later his guilt is by no means certain. He was found with a knife and was a fairly disreputable character, but neither of these would have marked him out from many residents in this part of London at this time in its history. He was also nothing like the description of the large man seen fleeing the scene by the Williamsons' lodger, being of medium height, slight build and altogether rather less substantial.

The authorities were nevertheless content that they had caught their man, and were thus shocked to hear that Williams had been found hanging in his cell when he was due to answer some more questions on 27 December. Suicide was at this time an illegal act, and by taking matters into his own hands Williams had also denied the courts and the public the opportunity to see justice being done.

In the absence of a usefully cathartic trial, it was therefore decided to parade his corpse through Wapping and Shadwell, in part to reassure the local population that it had no more to fear, but also in some way to avenge the dead. A procession duly set off on New Year's Eve, pausing for a few minutes at each crime scene and gradually attracting a crowd of more than 10,000 people who wished to enjoy the gruesome spectacle.

It had also been decided to give Williams a traditional suicide's burial; that is, one outside consecrated ground with a stake driven through the heart and the body buried without ceremony at a crossroads. (This was done in order to prevent the spirit finding its way home to haunt any former associates.) The chosen spot for the interment was at the junction of Cannon Street Road and Cable Street – immediately adjacent, as it happens, to where, just a few weeks previously, the Marr family had been buried in the shadow of Nicholas Hawksmoor's great church of St George's in the East.

HENRY WAINWRIGHT

Vine Court, E1 (1875)
40 Tredegar Square, E1 (1875)

'The Clearest and Most Convincing Evidence'

Living two lives simultaneously and at different addresses, 36-year-old Henry Wainwright was a successful commercial brush manufacturer, a respectable teetotal churchwarden living in tasteful comfort at No. 40 Tredegar Square and, by all accounts, a good father to his family. Unfortunately, had they but known it, Wainwright was also a serial philanderer who had fathered another two little girls who were living a mile and a half away and whose mother knew him as Percy King. He was not technically a bigamist, however, because although 'Mrs King' liked to be known as such, the two merely cohabited and she was in reality a hatmaker's assistant called Harriet Lane.

On 11 September 1875, Miss Lane was pronounced dead. The precise nature of her injuries, though, was obscured for the time being by the fact that she had been cut up into ten sections and bundled into a couple of hastily wrapped parcels. A year earlier, these had been buried beneath what is now Vine Court, but at the time was the yard of Wainwright's warehouse at No. 215 Whitechapel Road. Now renumbered No. 130, his business was conveniently located approximately halfway between his two otherwise unconnected lives, wives and families.

Wainwright's extraordinary double life, and indeed Harriet's murder, only came to light when a four-wheeled cab, or 'growler', called to carry the two parcels away from the warehouse the following year. Wainwright was having to move on, as financial troubles had forced him to surrender the lease on the premises. When the cabman arrived at the warehouse, one of the men working there was told to carry two foul-smelling parcels out to him. Poking around in one of them and finding what was clearly a human hand, the employee nevertheless did as he was told while deciding to follow the cab at a safe distance once his employer had climbed aboard.

Keeping out of sight, he followed the cab over London Bridge and all the way to an address near the Hop Exchange in Borough: only then was he able to alert a police constable to what he had found. Riding in the cab it was inevitable that the bearded, respectable and comfortably bourgeoise Wainwright should come under immediate suspicion, but his arrest must have proved profoundly shocking to his legitimate family and to those who moved in the same social, church and commercial circles.

It was soon revealed that the same money worries that had forced Wainwright's move from the warehouse (without which the victim's fate might still be unknown) had put pressure on his relationship with Harriet. Some months previously, he had moved her and the two girls into cheaper accommodation and reduced her allowance. Harriet took great exception to this and, being something of a drinker, when she voiced her objections rather too forcefully, 'Percy' had decided enough was enough.

After preparing a shallow grave behind the warehouse and procuring a gun, he had persuaded Harriet to visit the premises. On arrival she had been shot in the head, had her throat slit for good measure, and had been buried in the pit beneath a layer of disinfecting chloride of lime. With his brother's help, Wainwright had then concocted a story to cover her sudden disappearance, making it look as though Harriet was planning a trip to Paris with a purely fictional 'Mr Frieake'.

Incredibly, once in court, Wainwright had insisted that he had no idea what the parcels contained, and for a cash sum from a complete stranger he had simply agreed to store them for a while and later transport them across the river. The gun was shown to be his, however, and he had been caught in possession of the remains of his former lover. There was even a suggestion that he had attempted to bribe the policeman in Southwark rather than hand over the parcels. After being found guilty of the murder of Harriet Louisa Lane on what the judge called 'the clearest and most convincing evidence', Henry Wainwright was sentenced to be hanged on 21 December at Newgate Gaol.

The decision less than a decade earlier to stop executing criminals in public – the last in London had been that of the Fenian Michael Barrett on 26 May 1868 – might have led Wainwright to expect a dignified and private end. This was not to be, however, and the following day *The Times* was one of many newsapers to describe in detail the instrument of execution – 'peculiar in construction and appearance; it being roofed over, lighted with lamps at each end, and having a deep pit, over which a chain and noose were suspended' – as well as listing by name and rank the scores of city dignitaries who had shouldered their way into the yard at Newgate to see justice done by invitation of the Lord Mayor himself. Wainwright's execution had become one of the sights of London.

JACK THE RIPPER

Durward Street, E1 (1888)
Mitre Square, EC3 (1888)
Gunthorpe Street, E1 (1888)

Jack's Tracks Not so Easy to Follow

By far the most documented, yet still the most mysterious of capital killers, Jack was active for only a few months and his tally of five was awful but relatively modest. Yet no other serial killer has exercised quite such a hold on the British imagination nor garnered quite so many theories as to who was responsible, and how, precisely, he, she or they got away with it.

An internet search for the Ripper throws up literally millions of pages. New books, films, theories and even computer games on the subject are launched with metronomic regularity, and, nearly half a century after the last body was found, a successful wigmaker in Wardour Street was still advertising his business by claiming to have unwittingly provided Jack's disguise all those years before.

Jack the Ripper walks take place every week of the year in the relevant quarter of East London. These guided walks are incredibly popular, despite the fact that while we know who the victims were – Mary Ann Nichols, Annie Chapman, Elizabeth Stride, Catherine Eddowes and Mary Jane Kelly – and may even have memorised the minutiae of their pitiful injuries, all the locations but one have disappeared in the process of building, bombing, burning and rebuilding that has characterised city life over the last century.

Running off the high street in Whitechapel, one side of Gunthorpe Street with its arched entrance and cobbled surface still gives a fair impression of late 1880s London; indeed, the murder there of Martha Tabram on 7 August 1888 – in what was then called George Yard – has, by some historians, been added to Jack's tally. However, most research suggests we can only be sure about the five named on the previous page. Of these, the location of Mary Ann Nichols' killing, three weeks later, is the only one to bear much resemblance to its likely appearance on 31 August 1888. Back then, Durward Street was called Buck's Row, and the Board School is now apartments, but the small yard where the 41-year-old prostitute's body was discovered by Charles Cross in the early hours of the morning has survived more or less intact.

The same cannot be said for 29 Hanbury Street, a slum torn down in the 1960s, where the disembowelled body of Annie Chapman was found by one of its seventeen residents on 8 September. No one had heard a thing in the night and this second death ignited a panic in the area, with talk of the 'Whitechapel Murders' reaching fever pitch on the 30th with the discovery of a third mutilated body.

Elizabeth Stride's corpse was found on the site of what is now another school building in Henriques Street (then Berners Street), on the other side of Commercial Road. Less than an hour later, another gruesome discovery took Jack's total to four, this time being made within the historic City boundary. The body of Catherine Eddowes was found in Mitre Square (a colourful flower bed now marks the spot) and with scores of City of London Police now joining in the hunt, Jack appeared to have taken the decision to lay low for a while.

Perhaps because of this, it was to be 9 November before the fifth and final murder was discovered not far away in Miller's Court, the victim one Mary Jane Kelly. It was perhaps the worst of all, and was the only Ripper crime scene to be photographed; her mutilation was so complete as to render the corpse unrecognisable. The room itself – now lost beneath the City Corporation's multistorey car park on White's Row – was similarly so soaked in blood and gore that her landlord described the carnage as 'more like the work of a devil than the work of a man'.

Adding to the mystique that already surrounded the case, the killings then stopped as suddenly as they had started. Police continued to find clues chalked up on the walls around Whitechapel – many of them hoaxes and often implicating local Jews or Freemasons. Another two murders were subsequently attributed to Jack, although both have since been discounted.

Thereafter, the only other 'victim' in all this seemed to be Metropolitan Commissioner Sir Charles Warren, whose inability to find the killer led to him being forced out of office by public opinion. Also, in a sense, the victims included many who were rumoured to be Jack at the time but had no opportunity to clear their names. These included Seweryn Antonowicz Kłosowski (see p. 163), Thomas Neill Cream (p. 160) and even Walter Sickert (p. 139), all of whose names keep popping into the frame but without a shred of anything one might realistically term as evidence.

EDGAR EDWARDS

The Oliver Twist, 90 Church Road, E10 (1902)

'Now Get On With It, As Quick As You Like'

A couple of days before Christmas 1902, Edgar Edwards, who had a reputation as a shrewd if small-scale businessman, arranged to meet John Garland for a drink at his local on the corner of Church Road and Oliver Road. They were there to discuss a takeover of the latter's grocery firm, and after visiting the premises of the business they returned to the pub before continuing their negotiations at No. 89, where the 44-year-old Edwards was then living.

Within minutes Edwards had launched a vicious attack on Garland, which the victim subsequently described to an Old Bailey jury as 'absolutely unprovoked. He gave me a very severe blow, it almost knocked the senses out of me, and it was followed by a number of blows rained upon me while I was on the ground.'

Edwards soon found himself facing a charge of malicious wounding, but before this case could be heard he was under suspicion again. This time it was not for any violent altercation but rather after twice attempting to pass himself off under the name Darby. This was initially in connection with the purchase of another small business dealing in stationery and tobacconist's supplies, and the second time while pawning some small valuables.

Police decided to investigate further, and a search of No. 89 revealed some more pawn tickets in the name of Darby and some business cards. The latter led officers across the river to Camberwell and No. 22 Wyndham Road, the premises of another grocery business which Edwards was also apparently interested in buying.

The owners were John and Beatrice Darby, but neither they nor their 10-week-old baby daughter were to be seen at the address. Instead, on the mantelpiece in the back parlour, detectives found a lead weight of the sort used to counterbalance sash windows. This was covered with a quantity of blood and matted hair and, looking up, they found more blood oozing through the floorboards above.

Back in Leyton on 30 December, a workman was brought in to dig up a section of garden. He quickly uncovered six sacks and a small bundle, which were examined by the local divisional police surgeon. In these, the splendidly named Dr Jekyll reported, were found:

> ... the dismembered bodies of a man and woman, the heads and limbs had been cut off. I also saw the body of a child, which was intact. The heads were quite recognisable, the cause of death was due to injury to the heads in the cases of the man and woman, and in the case of the child to strangulation.

Extensive fractures to the adults' skulls and evidence of blows to the front and rear of their heads seemed to match the description of the type of furious onslaught inflicted on Garland. There seemed little, if any, doubt that Edgard Edwards was responsible and, having taken a liking to their business (after seeing an advertisement for it in the local press), he had decided to take their lives as well, thereby avoiding having to pay anything for the latter.

The following morning, he was duly charged with the wilful murder of William John Darby, Beatrice Darby and Ethel Beatrice, their child, on or about 29 November. This time he was taken into custody and remanded to Brixton Prison, with the case scheduled to be heard on 9 February.

Edwards refused to plead, so the court ordered a plea of not guilty to be entered for him, with the prisoner himself presumably hoping for a judgement that he was insane. However, this escape was denied by the prison medic James Scott. Although, rather oddly, he did feel the need to advise the court that having examined the prisoner, 'the shape of his head is somewhat peculiar'. Though finding no evidence of insanity, Scott restricted his diagnosis to a description of Edwards as 'mentally weak'.

Thereafter, with an abundance of evidence – some of it circumstantial, but plenty of it forensic – there seemed little question that Edwards would hang. Having shown himself to be both brutal and mercenary (court papers indicated that his rent on No. 89 was paid using the £7 raised by pawning a gold watch and a chain from Mr Darby), in the event he accepted his fate calmly. When a death sentence was passed, he told the court, 'Now get on with it, as quick as you like.'

'PETER THE PAINTER'

Cutler Street, E1 (1910)
Sidney Street, E1 (1910)

The Houndsditch Murders and the Siege of Sidney Street

On 16 December 1910, City of London Police were called to Houndsditch after neighbours heard what sounded like thieves attempting to break into the rear of a jeweller's shop, apparently by tunnelling into the shop from Exchange Buildings in the cul-de-sac behind. Nine police, both uniformed and plain-clothed, responded to the call-out. Three were fatally wounded and another two injured when they knocked on the door and attempted to enter.

Clearly the police had expected nowhere near this level of resistance, probably assuming they were simply interrupting an ambitious, if ham-fisted, attempt at burglary. But, in fact, the two gunmen and up to eight accomplices were members of the Latvian anarchist group Liesma, or the Gardstein Gang. Desperately needing to raise funds for their political struggle against Russian rule, they had alighted on the shop of H.S. Harris in the mistaken belief that the vault contained items belonging to the tsar.

Following what is still the bloodiest single-day assault on serving British police officers, the gang attempted to escape through the back of the premises. Emerging into Cutler Street and carrying one of their number whom they had shot by mistake, the gang eventually holed up at No. 59 Grove Road in Mile End. The wounded man died.

Amidst rumours that the gang was led by a notorious revolutionary known only as 'Peter the Painter', the police mounted a search of the area that continued over several weeks. Their lucky break came on 3 January when a tip-off led police to another house, at No. 100 Sidney Street, in which two or three gang members were said to be hiding. This time, one might have assumed the authorities would take no chances, but once again an unarmed officer was sent to knock on the door and, once again, he was answered by a hail of bullets.

The officer survived with no more than a punctured lung and an injured foot but, faced with an unknown number of assailants and with the police inadequately armed with a variety of bulldog revolvers, shotguns and rifles fitted with .22 Morristube barrels, an order for reinforcements was sent to St John's Wood barracks.

With a detachment of Scots Guards soon in attendance – and later the Home Secretary Winston Churchill, complete with top hat and cigar – what became known as the Siege of Sidney Street developed into a great public spectacle. Soon reporters were crowding into the area to get the story, and local householders were charging good money for a place on any rooftop with a reasonable view of the action.

Before long, soldiers, police and the gunmen were all trading fire. The question of tactics – as to who should get the honour of storming the building – was put on hold when smoke was observed pouring from the building. The fire brigade arrived but were told not to turn any hoses on the building, with Churchill perhaps being keen to flush out the gunmen like rats at stubble-burning time. In the end he relented, to save neighbouring properties, but only after the roof and upper floors of No. 100 had collapsed, thereby reducing the chance that anyone would be coming out alive.

Once the flames had died down, officers were able to enter the building but when they did so, only two bodies came to light: Fritz Svaars and William Sokolow. There was no sign of the mysterious Peter. The press lauded his ability yet again to somehow slip away unnoticed.

For months afterwards the newspapers traded stories of this elusive character: he had gone down with the *Lusitania* or had resurfaced in Moscow to lead the 1917 Bolshevik Revolution. The likelihood is that he never existed, and – much like the bullet rumoured to have creased Churchill's top hat that day – Peter was merely a press invention designed to enhance what was already quite a story.

Remarkably, given the size of the gang involved, no one ever stood trial for the attempted burglary at No. 119 Houndsditch, nor for the three murders that resulted from it. And while the police on that day could be forgiven for walking into such an ambush, the subsequent siege taught them a useful lesson: namely that as a force they were woefully ill-equipped when it came to dealing with a new generation of well-armed and sometimes dangerously effective criminals.

In 2010, to mark the 100th anniversary of their deaths, and with the jewellery shop long gone, a plaque was unveiled on a wall in Cutler Street in commemoration of sergeants Robert Bentley and Charles Tucker and PC Walter Choat.

More curiously, four years earlier, a Housing Trust block of flats in Sidney Street had been officially named Painter House after the elusive Peter – described on its commemorative plaque as an 'anti-hero' rather than a terrorist, armed robber and murderer – with 'Siege House' on the block next door ...

THE KRAY TWINS

Blind Beggar, 337 Whitechapel Road, E1 (1966)

'And There in Cold Blood Slay Another Human Being'

Step across Mile End Road from Sidney Street and it is hard to miss the Blind Beggar, a large and distinctive Victorian gin palace built in 1894 on the site of the old Mile End tollgate. As infamous these days as Rillington Place, the pub is where, on 9 March 1966, Ronnie Kray casually shot dead a rival gang member called George Cornell.

It was to be two years before he was arrested and sent down for this, and the papers the next morning made no mention of gang warfare, observing merely that 38-year-old Cornell, 'also known as Myers', hailed from Camberwell and had died on the operating table after being shot in the head. Nor was any particular connection made with the Blind Beggar, the scene of another murder some years previously when a man had been stabbed in the eye with a brolly.

Several witnesses had seen the shooting and would have been able to confirm what Cornell was drinking (a G&T) and even what record was playing on the jukebox at the time ('The Sun Ain't Gonna Shine Anymore' by the Walker Brothers). But no one was able to or wished to identify Ronnie Kray, who strolled out of the pub and into a waiting car that then drove him away.

When Ronnie and his brother were eventually arrested, on 8 May 1968, Cornell's murder was just one of the crimes of which they stood accused. For years, brief periods under arrest and incarceration had been punctuated by a series of criminal acts encompassing everything from arson to fraud, racketeering to hijacking, armed robbery and at least one other murder. (Lured to his death at Evering Road, Stoke Newington, in October 1967, Jack 'The Hat' McVitie had been repeatedly stabbed by Reggie, who was keen to demonstrate that he was his brother's equal.) The twins had also engaged in a long-running battle with their south London rivals, the Richardsons, whose associates included George Cornell.

Since they began in the 1950s, Ronnie, who is known to have suffered from paranoid schizophrenia, is said to have dreamed of committing the perfect crime, which for him was a Chicago gangster-style hit of the sort he attempted to pull off at the Blind Beggar. Calm, audacious, unhurried and – if only to those who inexplicably still hold a candle for the Krays – infinitely cool, Cornell's death was meant to demonstrate the twins' rise above mere criminality and their supposed supremacy over rival 'business' concerns.

Counting showbiz faces and political figures among their friends, famously photographed by David Bailey and inter-viewed on television, the Krays' loss of perspective is perhaps understandable, but no less risible for that. In court, things were quickly put back into context. Kenneth Jones QC for the prosecution described the 'horrifying effrontery, the deadly effrontery of two men who can walk into a public house in this land of ours on any evening and there in cold blood slay another human being'.

In order for their reign of terror to succeed, the twins, still in their mid-thirties at the time of their arrest, had relied on their ability to silence any opposition and to rule their streets through fear. But once the police finally went for them – Inspector Leonard 'Nipper' Read was allowed a team of twenty-seven to build a case – they found themselves on remand, whereupon witnesses slowly came forward and were persuaded to talk.

Ronnie may have been smart enough to leave no forensic evidence when he sauntered out of the Blind Beggar, but in court his getaway driver turned Queen's Evidence and identified Cornell's assailant by pointing out Reggie Kray and referring to 'the fat one with the glasses'. Another witness was able to testify that a total of three shots had been fired, one finding its mark on Cornell's forehead.

As the victim lay dying on the floor of the pub, the court heard, two men who had been drinking with him took to their heels, two more customers ducked out of sight, and the barmaid disappeared down into the cellar. In court she was identified only as 'Mrs X', a witness for the prosecution, and she admitted that she had not come forward earlier for fear that 'Ronnie would have shot me'.

Retiring for very nearly seven hours, the jury found her evidence compelling and dismissed the twins' appeals of innocence. The trial had lasted thirty-nine days in all – testing the endurance of everyone, according to the judge. Sentencing both to life imprisonment, Mr Justice Melford Stevenson patiently explained to the twins that 'in my view society has earned a rest from your activities'.

JULIUS STEPHEN

West Ham Station, E15 (1976)

A Rare Murder on the Underground

With an incredible billion passengers a year, eleven different lines, more than 250 miles of track and many hundreds of stations, besides being the world's oldest underground railway, the Tube is also among the biggest. Given this, it is inevitable that it would never remain a crime-free area, although most of the offences committed on the network are relatively minor, with approximately 550 thefts reported each year and some 200 incidents involving knives.

With the notable exception of large-scale terror outrages like the 7/7 attacks, deaths are still commendably rare. Of those that do occur, the vast majority are suicides, happening at a rate of approximately one a week and equivalent to the combined totals of the Paris Metro and New York Subway. The most popular time for jumping is 11 a.m., and the most popular stations are King's Cross and Victoria.

Among the better-known victims are Graham Bond (the eponymous Organisation's mellotron man) at Finsbury Park in 1974 and The Sound's Adrian Borland, who threw himself under a train at Wimbledon Station in 1999. Technically both were committing a criminal offence and, had they survived, they could have been charged with endangering safety on the railway and the obstruction of a train with intent.

A couple of years before Borland's death, the *Independent* ran a story concerning a worrying escalation in violence on the underground, after eight women had been held up at gunpoint. However, murders were still sufficiently rare to make that of Tube driver Julius Stephen especially noteworthy.

Back in 1914, the body of 7-year-old Margaret Nally had been found in the ladies' cloakroom at Aldersgate Street Station (now Barbican). She had been sexually assaulted and then suffocated using a piece of fabric pushed down her throat. Then, in 1957, Countess Teresa Lubienska, a Polish aristocrat, wartime resistance fighter and concentration camp survivor, was stabbed to death at Gloucester Road. On neither occasion was the murderer apprehended or identified.

The third death occurred on 15 March 1976 when 34-year-old Stephen, a West Indian Tube driver from Hammersmith, bravely gave chase after a gunman had detonated a bomb on his train. It is thought the 5lb bomb was intended to cause rush-hour panic at Liverpool Street Station, but the terrorist unwittingly got on a train heading the wrong way along what was then the Metropolitan Line.

Nine people were injured when it went off just moments after the train had left West Ham Station. Stephen was joined in the chase by 24-year-old Post Office Engineer Peter Chalk, who was working nearby: both were shot, with Stephen dying instantly, leaving a wife and young son.

This was the third such incident in recent weeks, but the only one to prove fatal. On 13 February, a much larger bomb had been defused at Oxford Circus Station, and on 4 March a 10lb device exploded in a carriage outside Cannon Street. Fortunately the train was empty, but eight passengers were injured on another train coming the other way. Shortly afterwards, armed plain-clothes policemen started patrolling the stations.

The gunman implicated in Stephen's killing was afterwards chased by police and turned his gun on himself when he was cornered. Using the usual circumlocutions, the BBC subsequently reported that 'armed detectives are currently guarding a man at Queen Mary's Hospital, West Ham'. The suspect was described as being in his mid-thirties, with an Irish accent and a London address.

Investigations subsequently revealed that the bomber had boarded an outward-bound train at Stepney Green, realising his mistake when the train surfaced at Plaistow – much of this stretch of what is now the Hammersmith & City Line is above ground – and swapping onto a train heading back into the centre. The mistake had badly upset his schedule. Injured, but not incapacitated by his own blast, he then attempted to escape through the driver's cab.

Other IRA attacks over the period were to prove yet more devastating and continued against even softer targets such as Harrods, a bandstand in Regent's Park and a ceremonial detachment of guardsmen from the Household Cavalry. The results were frequently horrendous, although London and Londoners proved their resilience again and again, and not for the last time the capital refused to be brought to its knees by terrorist gangs.

In 1977, a defendant at the Old Bailey received five life sentences for bombing a London Underground train, killing the driver and the attempted murder of another man, but was subsequently released as part of the 1998 Good Friday Agreement.

2

THE WEST END

SIR HENRY WILSON

36 Eaton Place, SW1 (1922)
Liverpool Street Station War Memorial (1922)

'The Foulest in the Foul Category of Irish Political Crimes'

Field Marshal Sir Henry Hughes Wilson, Bt GCB DSO MP remains the archetype of a certain class of public servant, born in Ireland and educated in England before embarking on an impressive military career serving the Empire. After failing repeatedly to win a place at either the Royal Military Academy at Woolwich or the junior establishment at Sandhurst, he joined a local militia before transferring in the 1880s to the more prestigious Rifle Brigade.

Service overseas followed, principally in Burma and India, with an injury leaving him walking with a stick for the remainder of his life. Returning to Britain, he worked in Intelligence at the War Office before being given the command of a battalion in his old brigade and later at Sandhurst.

His advancement during the Great War was equally impressive, Churchill recognising that in Wilson 'the War Cabinet found for the first time an expert adviser of superior intellect'. An enthusiast for a new species of armoured vehicles which was gradually supplanting the mounted horse, Churchill would have been delighted at Wilson's decision to more than double the size of the Tank Regiment.

Wilson was made a baronet after the Armistice and awarded £10,000 and the rank of field marshal by a grateful nation. He decided next to exchange military life for one in politics. In February 1922, he stood for Parliament and having won his seat accepted a new role a month later as security adviser to the new Northern Ireland Government.

Unfortunately, this brought Sir Henry into the sights of the London branch of the new IRA, an organisation which had grown out of the Easter Uprising and the Irish Volunteers. The London faction firmly opposed the Anglo-Irish Treaty, which the previous year had created the Irish Free State and numbered among its young firebrands Joseph O'Sullivan and Reginald Dunne, two 24-year-olds who had previously served in the British Army.

Discharged in 1917 on losing a leg at Ypres, O'Sullivan had been able to secure menial work at the Ministry of Munitions and may have been able to use his position to feed low-level intelligence back to his political masters. He was also implicated in the 1921 murder of Vincent Fovargue, an IRA informer who was found dead on a golf course near Staines with a label pinned to him reading, 'Let spies and traitors beware – IRA'.

In mid-June the following year, O'Sullivan and Dunne were informed that Sir Henry was due to unveil a new war memorial at Liverpool Street Station on 22 June. (This is still in situ, on a raised walkway adjacent to a branch of McDonald's.) The two men waited for him to return, and as Wilson approached the front door to his home in Eaton Place, he was shot three times and killed. A crowd quickly formed, and while attempting to escape the Irishmen fired again several times, injuring two policemen and a member of the public. With just the one leg, O'Sullivan made it only as far as Ebury Street before he was captured, as was Dunne when he turned back in a bid to help his friend.

Their weapons were quickly conveyed to the Cabinet Office at No. 10, and standing either side of the room's famous table Winston Churchill and Prime Minister Lloyd George silently contemplated the pistols that been used to take their colleague's life. Sir Henry's political career had been exceptionally short – his maiden speech to the House of Commons had been made just three months previously – but business in the chamber was adjourned immediately, and at Buckingham Palace a birthday banquet for the Prince of Wales was cancelled.

The two assassins refused to reveal their identities or occupations, and the following day the *Belfast Telegraph*, among others, named them as James Connolly and John O'Brien. Both were soon correctly identified, however, and after a short trial they were hanged on 10 August. A plaque was subsequently affixed to the aforementioned war memorial recording the murder of Sir Henry within two hours of the official unveiling ceremony.

Although Sir Henry was in some regards a logical target for such an outrage, O'Sullivan and Dunne's precise motives have never been explained. As the IRA was at this time deeply divided over whether or not to support the 1921 Treaty, it has been suggested that the assassination was intended to provoke the British into declaring war on Eire, thereby bringing the two sides together. In this at least, what *The Times* described as 'among the foulest in the foul category of Irish political crimes' must be adjudged to have failed.

ELVIRA BARNEY

21 William Mews, SW1 (1932)

'There was a Terrible Barney at No. 21'

The young socialite daughter of Sir John and Lady Mullen, Elvira Barney was separated from her musician husband and living the life in a tiny Knightsbridge mews house. In the early hours of 31 May 1932, the 27-year-old rang her doctor and asked him to come over. After being told only that there had been 'a terrible accident', Dr Thomas Durrant arrived to find the body of Michael Scott Stephen at the foot of the stairs. Stephen was three years younger than Elvira and very definitely dead from a gunshot wound to the chest.

Visibly upset and very agitated, Barney was at great pains to tell the doctor that as he lay dying Stephen had been saying, over and over, 'Why doesn't the doctor come? I want to tell him it was not your fault.' The accident, if indeed it was, had evidently involved a .32 Smith & Wesson revolver, which had clearly been fired at very close range and was now lying close to Stephen's body. A subsequent examination of the weapon revealed that two of its six chambers were empty.

Barney was arrested on suspicion of murder but told police that the gun had gone off accidentally during a struggle between the two of them. Stephen, she said, had threatened to kill himself with it. Neighbours in the narrow mews were able to confirm that the two had indeed been fighting. 'There was a terrible barney at No. 21' is how one of them put it – and it seemed this was a far from rare occurrence.

Apparently, the couple had returned home earlier in the evening from a party at the famous Café de Paris in Coventry Street near Leicester Square. One of their fights had started soon afterwards, with Mrs Barney at one point being heard to scream, 'Get out, get out of my house! I will shoot you! I will shoot you!' This had been followed by a loud bang – obviously the sound of the revolver going off – after which she was heard saying, 'Chicken, chicken, come back to me. I will do anything you want me to.'

A search of the premises revealed plenty of evidence of the couple's louche lifestyle; in particular, what the journalist Macdonald Hastings later memorably described as 'a wall painting which would have been a sensation in a brothel in Pompeii. The library was furnished with publications which could never have passed through His Majesty's Customs.' The house was equipped with what he describes as 'implements of fetishism and perversion' and it was known that the pair's lifestyle relied heavily on illegal stimulants, the provision of which had long been something of a Stephen speciality.

On 3 June, Barney was duly charged with Stephen's murder, but was allowed home to her parents' house at No. 6 Belgrave Square rather than being remanded in custody, as might have been the case had she not been so well connected socially. The trial, in which the society angle was bound to generate enormous public interest around the English-speaking world, was scheduled for 4 July.

At Westminster Police Court she was represented by none other than the Attorney General, Sir Patrick Hastings (no relation to Macdonald Hastings). His intention was to prove that the gun had gone off accidentally, despite a witness for the prosecution testifying to at least one other occasion on which Barney had shot at her lover in the street. Sir Patrick took the opportunity to demonstrate to the jury how the lack of a safety catch and an exceptionally light trigger action made an accidental firing more likely than not. After a summing up that the judge described as the best he had ever witnessed, Mrs Barney stepped out of the dock and slunk back into society.

Unfortunately for her, the verdict proved even more of a scandal than her lifestyle. Initially, the court of public opinion seemed satisfied, with crowds singing 'For She's a Jolly Good Fellow' outside the court, and bouquet after bouquet arriving at Belgrave Square. But the mood gradually turned against her, particularly when a report appeared in the press suggesting Mrs Barney had returned to the Café de Paris and, after a few too many, been heard to shout out, 'I am the one who shot her lover, so take a good look at me!'

Gradually, press interest in her waned, and she moved to France. On Christmas Day 1936, it was reported that Miss Elvira Mullen had been found dead in her hotel bedroom, collapsing after what had clearly been a quite riotous tour of the cafés and bars of Montmartre and the Latin Quarter.

More recently, permission was granted for the listed but dilapidated Manor House to be dismantled so the site could be developed.

LEOPOLD VON HOESCH

9 Carlton House Terrace, SW1 (1936)

London's Only Nazi Monument

In a tiny garden at the top of the Duke of York Steps in St James' is a carefully tended Nazi-era memorial. It looks out over a number of more imposing reminders of the British Empire, including monuments to Edward VII, Scott of the Antarctic, Sir John Franklin and even the Duke of Wellington, whose personal mounting block still stands outside the old United Service Club fronting onto Pall Mall.

Today the offending item is protected behind a sheet of glass, but it can still be read: '*Eine treuer Begleiter*' ('a true companion'). The reference is to a German Shepherd named Giro, who was buried here in February 1934 after making an impulsive connection with some exposed electrical wiring at the German Embassy next door. His master, Dr Leopold von Hoesch (1881–1936) was at the time German Ambassador to the Court of St James', which presumably explains the somewhat privileged location of Giro's final resting place.

In 1934, relations between Britain and Germany were cooling fast, with international opinion still more wary than openly warlike, although Hitler was fast consolidating his grip on power. In fact, von Hoesch was an unenthusiastic Nazi himself, and having played a significant role in normalising relations between the Great War powers and his own defeated nation, he was regarded as a statesman of both skill and charm.

A popular figure on the London scene, who could count a number of senior British politicians as friends, his sudden death in 1936 was potentially a blow to relations between the two countries. Because of this, and in line with normal protocols for an ambassador dying in office, von Hoesch was accorded what amounted to a state funeral before he left London for the last time. This included a nineteen-gun salute, a detachment of Grenadier Guards marching alongside Nazi troops accompanying the ceremonial gun limber on which his swastika-draped coffin was borne to Victoria Station, and a phalanx of British Cabinet ministers on hand to lead the mourners.

Officially von Hoesch had died of a stroke, which was unusual but by no means unprecedented for a man in his mid-fifties. However, the arrival of his replacement the following October, the reviled Joachim von Ribbentrop, who was to cause a scandal by greeting King George VI with a straight-armed '*Sieg Heil*', raised suspicions in both political and social circles that Giro's master had more likely been deliberately bumped off.

Never a supporter of Ribbentrop and dismissive of his erratic behaviour and arrogant and tactless methods, von Hoesch had frequently criticised him in despatches back home. He would doubtless have agreed with an assessment made sixty years later by the historian Lawrence Rees labelling Ribbentrop 'the Nazi almost all the other Nazis hated'. Unfortunately, however, with Hitler in power it was very much Ribbentrop's star that was in the ascendant rather than von Hoesch's.

The latter's patriotism was never in doubt, but neither was his antipathy towards the extremes of Nazism; discharging what he saw as his responsibilities as ambassador on a number of occasions brought him into dangerous conflict with his increasingly powerful rival. For example, memoranda drafted by him and transmitted to Berlin correctly warned that the opinions of some of Ribbentrop's most prized contacts – who were to include George Bernard Shaw, Sir Austen Chamberlain and the marquesses of Lothian and Londonderry – could no longer be regarded as representative of the true direction or strength of British feeling towards Germany. At the same time, his claim that German remilitarisation of the Rhineland in March 1936 would inflame French and British opinion, making another war more not less likely, was bound to infuriate the Führer for whom it was a vital strategic move (and one he had argued for in the pages of *Mein Kampf*).

Given all this, von Hoesch could not have been allowed to remain in post and his timely death avoided any diplomatic complications that might have resulted from his being recalled. His murder would not have been difficult to arrange nor to cover up, because the British authorities had no right to examine the body as the embassy, like others, was technically foreign sovereign territory. The cover story of a stroke or heart attack would also save his family from dishonour or further persecution by the Nazis.

As a footnote, it is curious to note that although many buildings and memorials in the surrounding area suffered very considerable damage at the hands of Luftwaffe, and given the natural antipathy towards Germany at this time, Giro's grave somehow came through the war unscathed. A stroke of good fortune, but also, perhaps, an unusual tribute to Britain's well-advertised love of dogs.

SHAHEED UDHAM SINGH

10 Caxton Street, SW1 (1940)

'I Did It Because I Had a Grudge Against Him. He Deserved it.'

As Lieutenant Governor of the Punjab during Lord Chelmsford's viceroyalty, Sir Michael O'Dwyer's error was to approve the massacre of up to 1,000 unarmed Indian subjects at Amritsar, with many more than that number injured. His published description of the action as 'correct' rebounded on him more than twenty years later when he was shot dead inside what is now an unusually ornate Victorian apartment block close to New Scotland Yard.

The building was once Caxton Hall, which was for decades the register office of choice for celebrity marriages, including those of Peter Sellers, Elizabeth Taylor, Ingrid Bergman, Yehudi Menuhin, Ringo Starr and Mick Jagger. Its proximity to Westminster meant it was also an important place for protest and lobby groups such as the Suffragettes to gather and somewhere for rallies and meetings intended to further various diverse political aims.

On 13 March 1940, Sir Michael was booked to address a conference held there under the auspices of the East India Association and the Royal Central Asian Society. This was also where he was to meet his nemesis, a fanatical but patient supporter of the Indian independence movement called Shaheed Udham Singh.

The aforementioned massacre in the gardens of Jallianwala Bagh on 13 April 1919 had proved a turning point in Singh's life, an event he witnessed personally when thousands of protesters were confronted by a small detachment of British troops under Brigadier General Reginald Dyer. Dyer's troops numbered fewer than 100 but were equipped with the latest model of Enfield rifle. They opened fire and continued to fire until their ammunition was exhausted.

Throughout the incident Dyer ordered his men to fire low, which is to say not over the protesters' heads, and also deliberately directed the fusillade to those places where the crowd was thickest. Witnesses later asserted that latterly much of the fire had been concentrated on the exits from the gardens, thereby preventing anyone escaping what quickly became a hail of death.

The Indian National Conference subsequently claimed there were 1,000 dead and 1,500 injured, figures which the official British report rejected in favour of 379 dead with 1,100 injured. However, even these were considered too shocking for home consumption and were suppressed, together with a cable to Dyer from O'Dwyer congratulating him on preventing a revolution.

Unfortunately, an official Committee of Enquiry found no evidence of such a revolution, and described as grave a number of errors, including the lack of warning given and the duration of fire. O'Dwyer nevertheless stuck to his guns and in his memoirs insisted that following this punishment, 'the Punjabis were quick to take to heart the lessons that revolution is a dangerous thing'.

This was clearly very far from the truth, in that the events of that day did nothing to slow demands in India for independence. Back home, Dyer was rewarded with a cash bounty by readers of one singularly pro-Empire British paper, but he was also thereafter branded the 'Butcher of Amritsar', with members on both sides of the House of Commons expressing their regret and revulsion at what had occurred.

Back in India, for one witness the national pain and humiliation proved too much to bear. After visiting the nearby Harmandir Sahib (Golden Temple), Udham Singh made a vow to join the struggle for Punjabi and Indian independence and, in time, to take revenge on those he felt were responsible.

Due to a spell in jail for possession of unlicensed weapons and ammunition, it was to be a decade and a half before he reached London. He moved into 9 Adler Street, which ran between Whitechapel and Commercial roads, and later to an address in Mornington Crescent. He managed to buy a .45 calibre revolver and some ill-matched rounds from a soldier in a pub and decided to bide his time and wait for an occasion when he could kill O'Dwyer and make the maximum impact.

The Caxton Hall meeting provided him with the perfect opportunity, and with the gun hidden in a book he had specially hollowed out for the purpose, Singh waited until the end of the meeting before opening fire. After killing his quarry and injuring the Indian Secretary of State and two others, he made no attempt at escape, instead admitting that he had done it 'because I had a grudge against him, he deserved it. I don't belong to any society or anything else. I don't care, I don't mind dying.'

Requesting only that his remains be returned to the Punjab – which was to be denied for another thirty-four years – Shaheed Udham Singh refused to plead in court and was hanged at Pentonville Prison on 31 July 1940.

THE 7TH EARL OF LUCAN

46 Lower Belgrave Street, SW1 (1974)
Plumber's Arms, Lower Belgrave Street, SW1
(1974)

'Murder, There's Been a Murder!'

When the Countess of Lucan rushed into a popular Belgravia pub on 7 November 1974 shouting these words, she was dressed in nightclothes and bleeding heavily from a head wound. The phrase sparked a national manhunt and launched one of the most extraordinary narratives of any twentieth-century English killer.

The focus of police enquiries was and remains her estranged husband, the 7th Earl Richard John Bingham. At that time, the Old Etonian lived a few minutes' walk away at No. 72a Elizabeth Street. He was a committed but largely unsuccessful gambler – despite his nickname 'Lucky', the family silver was long gone. He had apparently let himself into the family home in Lower Belgrave Street and, some time after 9 p.m., attacked the children's new nanny, Mrs Sandra Rivett. The 40-year-old peer is widely assumed to have been after his wife, who he blamed for the break-up of his marriage, the loss of custody of his children and possibly somehow even his rising gambling debts.

Rather than some splendid Palladian pile set among rolling acres, No. 46 was a smart but discreet terraced house typical of this part of the Duke of Westminster's London estate, but by no means one of the large ones. In most other regards, though, the killing had all the hallmarks of a round of Cluedo, from the titled prime suspect to his choice of weapon, a short length of lead piping. This aspect of the case, and the fact that Lucan subsequently managed to disappear into thin air, has done much to account for its subsequent notoriety.

There were rumours that he had been spirited out of the country by rich and powerful friends. His passport was left behind at Elizabeth Street and a borrowed car was abandoned in Newhaven. Since then he has been seen (often simultaneously) in South Africa, India, Ireland, Australia, Gibraltar and even the Netherlands.

The likelihood, however, is that the former guards officer is dead and has been for a long time. There are plenty of websites and internet forums advancing the opposing view, but nothing about Lucan's lifestyle in the run-up to his disappearance suggests he was heading for a long, healthy retirement. Nor indeed that he might have the personal resources necessary to carve out a new life once he had exiled himself from the privileged and somewhat cloistered clubland existence he had hitherto enjoyed.

In any event, while the lack of a body means no death certificate can be issued, he has long since been declared dead. On 11 December 1992, Lucan was 'presumed deceased in chambers', and then on 11 August 1999 a grant issued by the High Court of Justice stated unequivocally, 'BE IT KNOWN that the Right Honourable RICHARD JOHN BINGHAM 7th Earl of Lucan of 72a Elizabeth Street London SW1 died on or since the 8th day of November 1974.'

When the Ford Corsair he had been driving that night was found in Newhaven, the upholstery was bloodstained and a length of lead piping found in the boot wrapped in surgical tape matched the one found in Lower Belgrave Street. His disappearance already looked highly suspicious, and this grisly discovery was enough for the police to issue an arrest warrant immediately.

Interestingly, it was also enough to have His Lordship pronounced guilty, albeit not at the Old Bailey after a conventional trial by jury but in the Coroner's Court. An inquest held in June 1975 unanimously named the 7th Earl the murderer of Mrs Rivett. This was the very last occasion on which this was allowed to happen as an inquest's right to name an individual as a murderer was shortly afterwards abolished by the Criminal Law Act (1977).

That said, and aside from the fact that no body has ever surfaced, a number of unanswered questions continue to keep the case alive in the public's imagination. Lucan was clearly a troubled individual under mounting pressure, and his behaviour was increasingly erratic. But few who knew him personally seemed to have thought him capable of murder or considered him impulsive enough to launch such a violent and bloody attack without assessing the consequences. It seems clear that he had made no real plans for an escape. However, for many this just makes Lucan's successful disappearing act all the more impressive. For others, it simply suggests that, having dumped the car at Newhaven and realising the game was up almost immediately, the hapless peer perhaps jumped off a ferry and drowned ...

ALEXANDER LITVINENKO

Millennium Hotel, 44 Grosvenor Square, W1
(2006)
Ishi, 167 Piccadilly, W1 (2006)

'Intrigue, Betrayal and Ruthless Trickery were the Tools of Working Life'

When a smart West End hotel and a branch of a well-known sushi chain sparked a public health alert in November 2006 with traces of a deadly radioactive isotope being found at both premises, talk of a connection between the death of a dissident and former KGB agent sounded like something from the pages of an espionage novel. The scare led to several hundred Londoners being tested for the effects of radiation.

However, the real victim was Alexander Litvinenko. The 43-year-old had fled Russia after working for eighteen years at the KGB and its successor organisations, the FSK and FSB, having acquired a reputation since then as something of a thorn in the side of the authorities in his home country.

As the *Independent* was to put it following his death at University College Hospital on 23 November, Litvinenko 'occupied a world where intrigue, betrayal and ruthless trickery were the tools of working life'. In that regard, his death should perhaps not have caused the media ripple it did – as one who seemed to live by the sword, his end might have been foreseen with a certain inevitability.

The presumed presence of a foreign hitman in London was bound to attract press interest, however, as indeed was the choice of weapon: a hitherto little-known heavy metal called Polonium 210. There were also plenty of rumours doing the rounds that the hit had been officially sanctioned by the state rather than being carried out by renegade agents or the so-called Russian mafia.

While it remains highly unlikely that such a thing will ever be proven, it was always clear that Litvinenko had done little to appease his enemies in Russia since arriving in England to claim asylum in 2000. He had first come to prominence two years earlier after exposing an alleged plot to assassinate another erstwhile Kremlin insider, Boris Berezovsky, who had amassed a huge fortune before moving to Britain and spending quite a chunk of it on a large house in Surrey which had previously been owned by DJ Chris Evans. Following the exposure, Litvinenko had been arrested on charges of abusing his office by exceeding his authority. He was eventually acquitted of the charge but not before spending nine months in custody.

His next brush with the law came with the publication of a book, *Blowing up Russia: Terror from Within*, in which he claimed that atrocities blamed on Chechen separatists were actually the work of the Russian Federal Security Service (FSB). Accusing its agents of killing more than 300 citizens this way, Litvinenko also alleged that the agency had been training Al-Qaeda No. 2, Ayman al-Zawahiri in Dagestan before the events of 9/11.

By late 2006, Litvinenko had moved on and was investigating the case of Anna Politkovskaya, a journalist whose enquiries into high-level corruption had been linked to her own murder in October that year. Just weeks after showing an interest in her death, Litvinenko was himself taken ill, his physical decline so rapid that within days a man who prided himself on running several miles a day was photographed in a hospital bed: bald, deathly pale and unable to rise.

Still able at least to communicate effectively, Litvinenko described to police his recent movements. By tracking his progress from one appointment to another over the preceding couple of days, traces of the deadly radionuclide were discovered at several London addresses. These included Litvinenko's own home at No. 140 Osier Crescent in Muswell Hill but also several commercial premises; clearly aware of the methods employed by those active in the shadowy intelligence underworld, Litvinenko preferred to meet contacts at busy public locations.

A BBC timeline of Litvinenko's movements in the run-up to his death, describing a meeting in Grosvenor Square with a former KGB colleague and a visit to the sushi bar on Piccadilly, reads like something from a John le Carré novel, with the victim being admitted to one hospital and then transferred to another under heavy police guard. When his death was finally announced the cause was put down first to a mysterious toxic substance but then to acute radiation poisoning, making Alexander Litvinenko the first ever victim of nuclear terrorism.

The same BBC report also revealed that traces of radioactivity had been found at Heathrow – Home Secretary John Reid confirming that two Russian aircraft were 'of interest' – but four days later, after British detectives had travelled to Moscow, the Russian Prosecutor General Yuri Chaika stated categorically that no one would be extradited to Britain in connection with the poisoning. Instead, four diplomats were expelled from Britain, with Russia responding with a similar gesture seventy-two hours later.

3

ON THE RIVER

FREDDIE MILLS

Hammersmith Bridge, W6 (1964)

Was He Jack the Stripper?

While the perpetrator has yet to be determined with any certainty, Londoners in the 1960s were gripped by a series of killings variously known as the Hammersmith or Nude Murders, when six bodies were discovered along the western reaches of the London Thames over a period of barely more than a year. The first body, belonging to 30-year-old Hannah Tailford, was found near Hammersmith Bridge on 2 February 1964 with her underwear rammed down her throat.

All the victims were working girls – two with a tangential connection to the previous year's Profumo Scandal – and all six of them had been strangled or choked while having sex. Their naked bodies were then dumped on waste ground or along the Thames shore by a mystery killer, who the press promptly dubbed 'Jack the Stripper'. No one was ever charged with any of the murders (or placed in connection with two superficially similar killings a few years earlier), although the name of boxer Freddie Mills came into the frame after his own death in July 1965.

Not long after the discovery of the last body, Mills had been found shot through the eye in his own car with a fairground rifle propped up between his legs. It was an unusual injury for a suicide (particularly as the eye is thought to have been open when the gun went off), although this was the official verdict. The car was parked in Goslett Yard off the Charing Cross Road, close to the Chinese restaurant in which the 1948 light-heavyweight world champion had invested much of his winnings from a successful career as a popular pugilist and fight promoter.

His death was always controversial, however, with family and friends (including several minor celebrities and some major criminals) insisting that suicide was just not in Freddie's make-up. Faced with this uncertainty, the rumour mill ground into action to fill the vacuum, with unsubstantiated claims quickly being made that Freddie, a family man, was up on an indecency charge in a public lavatory; he had been bumped off by Chinese Triads wishing to move in on his Soho business interests; and he had had an affair with Ronnie Kray.

For now, all this was still in the future. With the death count piling up along the river, the police launched a huge inquiry. After interviewing some 7,000 individuals, Scotland Yard eventually announced that the number of suspects had been reduced to fewer than two dozen. Shortly afterwards, this number was revised downwards to ten and then three, after which the killings ceased as abruptly as they had begun.

An observer might suggest that on watching the odds of his being caught shortening so dramatically, perhaps the killer had sensibly decided to call it a day. The reality, however, is that serial killers seem rarely, if ever, able to control their urges to kill in this way, and because of this it is thought highly unlikely that such a prolific and brutal murderer could simply have melted into the background by returning to a more law-abiding life.

Instead, it was thought that the killer might have chosen to take his own life, and certainly at the time a security guard working close to where the sixth girl was found came under suspicion after committing suicide. Subsequently, it emerged that he was in Scotland at the time of at least one of the killings, which may explain why Mills came back into the frame.

It surfaced again most recently in 2001 in an *Observer* article by the paper's crime correspondent, Tony Thompson. The story, headlined 'Boxing Hero Freddie Mills "murdered eight women"', referred to the book *South London Gangster* in which Mills emerges as 'a vicious serial killer, responsible for the brutal deaths of at least eight young women whose naked bodies were found in or around the River Thames'. The author, Jimmy Tippett, interviewed several generations of east and south London 'faces', many of whom were known to him personally, and concluded that Mills, perhaps fearful that the police were closing in on him, decided to take his own life rather than risking the drop. By disguising it as a hit, he may have hoped to save his family's feelings.

The case is still very far from closed, however, as other candidates have emerged in recent years, including a deceased detective chief superintendent (in Jimmy Evans and Martin Short's book *The Survivor*), and in David Seabrook's *Jack of Jumps*, another writer with a particular interest in the subject, who is also now dead. Nearly half a century on, however, the probability must be that we shall never know for sure.

GEORGI MARKOV

Waterloo Bridge, SE1 (1978)

London's Notorious 'Umbrella Murder'

On 7 September 1978, while waiting at a bus stop at the southern end of Waterloo Bridge, broadcast journalist and Bulgarian dissident writer Georgi Ivanov Markov felt a momentary discomfort on the back of one leg. It was reportedly no more than an insect bite or sting and he continued on his journey across the river to his work at the BBC World Service.

At first, he assumed he had simply been accidentally jostled by the rush-hour crowds – a pedestrian had even apologised for bumping into him – but four days later he was pronounced dead, having developed a fever the first night and alerting the police to his suspicion that he had been poisoned. In particular, he was able to tell them that after feeling the slight sting, he had noticed a man hurrying off in the opposite direction after picking up an umbrella which had fallen to the ground. Also, on arrival at the BBC he had found a small red pimple on the back of his right leg. The two, he felt sure, were not unconnected.

A high-profile Communist exile and thus a definite candidate for the at-risk register, Markov had already received several death threats. Police were also aware that he ate only home-cooked meals, having been warned in an anonymous telephone call that he would eventually be poisoned. It was also noted that

7 September was the birthday of Todor Zhivkov, the Bulgarian leader.

Taking the dead man at his word, police requested a detailed examination of the 49-year-old's body and pathologists soon discovered a tiny spherical metal pellet embedded in Markov's calf. No larger than a pinhead and made of an unusual platinum-iridium alloy, this had been hollowed out and still contained minute traces of a sugary compound together with some ricin, a poison for which there is no antidote.

Experts at Porton Down, the top-secret government laboratory in Wiltshire, thought it likely that the sugary substance was used to seal the cavity. Carefully formulated to melt at precisely 37°C, it would then enable the release of the ricin into the victim's bloodstream once the pellet had reached human body temperature.

Markov's death read like a piece of spy theatre, worthy of Bond at his best. An unknown assassin striking in the midst of a crowd, the murder weapon an ordinary-looking umbrella specially modified for just such a purpose, and the highly toxic ammunition almost too small to see and, in any event, even if found, impossible to disable.

In one sense, the mystery had already been solved before Markov had even died. Broadcasting on the BBC World Service, America's Radio Free Europe and Deutsche Welle in Germany, Markov was so often critical of the Bulgarian regime that many of his fellow commuters just assumed the Bulgarian Government had decided to rid itself of him, possibly with the connivance of the KGB. But the identity of the actual killer took many years to emerge, and did so only after the fall of the Berlin Wall and the subsequent upheavals. Even then, the story that emerged was as tangled as any espionage thriller, with plenty of scope for a sequel.

In 1992, a former Bulgarian secret police chief received a ten-month sentence for deliberately destroying files on the Markov case. His boss, Deputy Interior Minister General Stoyan Savov, was also due to stand trial on related charges but committed suicide after a search of Bulgaria's secret service HQ had uncovered a stash of similarly customised umbrellas. It was widely reported at the time that these had indeed been devised by the KGB, which had also supplied the ricin-filled pellets, although with the destruction of so much paperwork the proof of this may never be found.

Further research did indicate, however, that the Markov job had been subcontracted out to a Danish hitman of Italian extraction, codenamed 'Piccadilly'. Here was a mysterious figure who had spent much of the 1970s travelling round Europe in a caravan under the cover of being an art dealer. He is known to have been used for specific jobs by the Bulgarian authorities and in 2005 was named by the *Sunday Times* as Markov's killer. The paper also described an almost identical attack on a second Bulgarian broadcaster, Vladimir Kostov, who had survived thanks to a thick woollen garment which prevented the toxin from properly penetrating his skin.

'Piccadilly' is known to have made three trips to London in 1977 and 1978. He was the only Bulgarian agent active in the city at that time and flew out the very day after Markov was hit. He has not been seen publicly since 1993, when his house in Denmark was put on the market – and his current whereabouts are still unknown.

ROBERTO CALVI

Blackfriars Bridge, EC4 (1982)

'Where the Tide Ebbs and Flows Twice in Twenty-Four Hours'

Found hanging from Blackfriars Bridge after the collapse of Italy's Banco Ambrosiano, the death of Calvi – immortalised in Fleet Street as 'God's Banker' – was clearly intended to look like suicide. It was, nevertheless, widely assumed to be an assassination, although it was to take a full decade before an official inquiry reached a similar judgement, and twenty-three years before anyone stood trial on such a charge.

Calvi reportedly had drugs in his system and pockets weighted down with bricks, but as a suicide it raised a number of questions, appearing somewhat too elaborate – why did he not just jump into the river? – and strangely public for someone who presumably could have just taken an overdose at his comfortable home in Hampstead.

Interest in the case blossomed when it emerged that Calvi, chairman of the Milan branch of what had been his country's largest private bank, was a member of Italy's controversial *Propaganda Due* or P2. This was a socially prestigious and highly secretive Masonic organisation, favoured by Establishment figures such as politicians, newspaper editors, military officers and civil servants from the upper echelons.

After links were made between this so-called 'black' lodge and a number of financial and corruption scandals, in addition to the collapse of the Banco Ambrosiano, the official Italian Masonry was quick to distance itself, pointing out that P2's charter had been withdrawn as long ago as 1976. The conspiracy theorists had long since stopped listening, however, and for them Calvi's death over water appeared deeply significant, symbolic of an ancient punishment designed to warn other members of the brotherhood from transgressing. For evidence of this, they cited an ancient text, the first of the Masons' three blood oaths:

O that my throat had been cut across, my tongue torn out, and my body buried in the rough sands of the sea, at low water mark, where the tide ebbs and flows twice in twenty-four hours ...

Calvi had been found on 19 June, nine days after fleeing Milan via Venice. A passer-by spotted his body hanging from the scaffolding under the bridge. Already implicated in what the BBC characterised as a 'complex web of international fraud and intrigue', and with a $400 million hole in the bank's accounts, Calvi was found to be carrying more than $14,000 in three different currencies. A verdict of suicide was reached at the inquest, which was held the following month, when it was also noted that Calvi had shaved off his moustache, presumably in a half-hearted bid to disguise his identity.

It is true he had attempted suicide once before, in prison in Italy in 1981, before being released on appeal in a case involving the illegal export of several billion lire. But the London judgement was soon overturned, at first with an open verdict and then in 2002 by a conclusion that he had been murdered. This was reached after forensic experts appointed by the Italian courts were able to demonstrate that Calvi's neck showed none of the injuries usually associated with a death by hanging, and that his hands had not come into contact with the bricks in his pockets. They also insisted that there was no evidence on Mr Calvi's shoes or clothing to suggest that he had climbed the scaffolding, indicating that he had been killed elsewhere.

Another two years passed before the BBC reported that four people – one already serving two life sentences – had been charged in connection with the killing and that they would be going on trial in Italy. With the case expected to expose Mafia or other underworld connections to various financial scandals, the BBC's Tamsin Smith confirmed that prosecutors would be attempting to prove that Calvi had been killed in order to prevent him revealing explosive secrets about Italy's political and religious establishment. At the same time, it was suggested that mob bosses might have been concerned that Calvi, knowing where their money was hidden, would reveal this in the hope of reducing his sentence.

The trial duly opened in Rome in October 2005 – by which time a fifth defendant had joined the others in the dock – but in June 2007, after the jury had retired to consider its verdict, all five were acquitted. Since then no one else has stood trial for Calvi's murder.

After so many years co-operating with the Italian authorities, the City of London Police expressed their disappointment at the judgement 'for Roberto Calvi's family in particular, that those responsible for his murder have still not faced justice'. But their concern must also have been that, once again, the tentacles of a foreign criminal power had reached deep into the capital and managed to escape after carrying out a brutal extrajudicial killing on the streets of London.

As for the scene of Calvi's death, at the time of writing this was undergoing a dramatic change with the development of a new railway station being built out over the river as part of the adjacent Blackfriars rail bridge.

'ADAM'

Tower Bridge, EC3 (2001)
The Globe, SE1

'... Like Some Element of Ritualism is Involved'

Around fifty bodies a year are pulled from the Thames, of which approximately four-fifths are suicides, most of whom will have jumped off a bridge. Most occur during the winter months, with a peak around Christmas, and in summer the occasional drunk jumps in without considering the consequences. The rest are assumed to have been murdered.

The unenviable task of recovering the bodies falls to the Marine Support Unit, the old Thames Division with its mortuary facility at Wapping Police Station. Those found are held for identification in a tank covered by a blue tarpaulin which is visible from passing pleasure boats. Each one is labelled DB1, DB2, etc. – shorthand for 'Dead Body', with the numbers being reset to 1 every New Year's Day.

Occasionally officers choose something slightly more personal, as was the case with the torso found floating close to Tower Bridge on 21 September 2001. It belonged to a little boy who was thought to have been 5 or 6 years old when he died and, suspecting that his death had some ritualistic element to it, police investigating the case named him 'Adam'.

Adam's remains were spotted by a pedestrian on the bridge, floating upstream in the direction of the Tate Modern and the Globe Theatre. He was thought to have been in the water for up to ten days. This in itself is not unusual: it can frequently take two to three weeks for a body to be recovered, by which time it can be in a dreadful state, not least because, as a river policeman once put it, 'the water is very cruel, the river is tidal, you get hit by boats and barges and attacked by seabirds'.

The grim discovery of Adam, together with a quantity of half-burned candles on the foreshore, wrapped in cloth bearing a common African name, Adekoyejo Fola Adeoye, led to stories in the press of ritual murder and 'voodoo killings'. Pollen in the victim's lungs indicated that he had been in London for at least seventy-two hours, but the suspicion was that he had been brought there expressly to be killed. Toxicology reports also showed that he had been alive but paralysed at the moment when his throat was cut.

When the torso was pulled from the water it was dressed only in a pair of orange shorts, of a type sold by Woolworths in Germany and Austria. For now, nothing else about Adam's identity could be determined with any certainty. Mineral and vegetable matter found in his stomach included minute particles of bone and gold, suggesting that Adam had been a victim of the sort of 'Muti' killing known to take place in many parts of sub-Saharan Africa. Pioneering work on radio isotopes found in all human bone later narrowed it down by providing a link to the geology of a particular area of south-west Nigeria close to Benin City and Ibadan.

Such ritualised murders are usually carried out in the belief that the bodies of particular children are sacred, with the remains frequently being disposed of in flowing water. Thereafter, certain body parts command huge sums for use in primitive rituals and medicines, and are said to bring good luck, sexual virility and success in business. It is rare in Africa, and never before seen in England, although a couple of similar killings had recently come to light in Germany and Belgium according to newspaper reports.

In 2003, police working on Adam's case announced they had arrested twenty-one people in raids on nine London addresses involving more than 200 officers. Most of the ten men and eleven women were arrested for immigration offences, identity fraud and passport forgery, but the BBC reported the discovery of a number of items which, according to the Met's Commander Andy Baker, 'would raise a few eyebrows. They look like some element of ritualism is involved.'

Another suspect was subsequently jailed for child trafficking but no charges specific to the torso followed the raids, and after another three years of investigations the police seemed to have drawn a blank. Adam was finally laid to rest in an unmarked grave somewhere in London. It was, a police spokesman told the BBC, 'a sad, thoughtful and dignified service to celebrate Adam's short life' and was attended only by those closely involved in the case.

A decade on, police still had little more to report beyond the hope that the enormous publicity surrounding the case would dissuade others from attempting something similar. Then, in late 2012, detectives involved in the case described as a 'major breakthrough' the news that an apparently reliable witness could identify the torso as belonging to a child called Patrick Erhabor. A retired police chief inspector who had worked on the original investigation told the *Daily Mail*, 'Without a name murders are very hard to solve. This is a crucial starting point for us and it should lead us to who killed him.' Even so, nearly three years later, the case was still unsolved.

4

BLOOMSBURY TO COVENT GARDEN

WILLIAM TERRISS

Adelphi Theatre, Stage Door,
Maiden Lane, WC2 (1897)

'If He is Dead, He Knew
What to Expect from Me'

Among the many unexplained presences that have been reported on the London Underground – at least a dozen stations from Aldgate to Ickenham are said to be haunted – is a ghostly character who has been seen stalking the tunnels and platforms at Covent Garden. An imposing figure in a frock coat, tall hat, glasses and gloves, the apparition was first recorded in 1928 and then again in the 1950s, when it was suggested it could be the ghost of a Victorian actor who appeared on stage under the name William Terriss.

Terriss was born William Charles Lewin in 1847, leaving Jesus College, Oxford, without graduating and trying his hand at several different careers around the world. These included sheep farming Down Under, tea planting in the subcontinent, prospecting for precious metals in the Americas and even medicine, before Terriss eventually decided to return home and take to the stage.

His energy, adventurous personality and naturally swashbuckling demeanour seemed to stand him in good stead professionally, and a run of popular and remunerative appearances followed in shows based on such box office favourites as

Ivanhoe and *Robin Hood*. Terriss also took on Shakespeare, playing Cassio in *Othello* and eventually the lead in *Romeo and Juliet*.

In a short and risky business Terriss proved to be a success and, after touring the USA in a number of productions in 1885 with his lover Jessie Millward, he returned to London where he was rarely without work. He also married well, to a fellow professional, producing a son Tom (who followed his parents into the business to become an actor, writer and later a film director) and a daughter Ellaline (who married the theatre proprietor Seymour Hicks).

Seymour Hicks owned two theatres in the West End, and at one of these – the Adelphi – his father-in-law was booked in December 1897 to appear in William Gillette's melodrama, *Secret Service*. Terriss arrived there for work as usual on the evening of 16 December, but on stepping up to what is now the stage door on Maiden Lane he was violently accosted by Richard Prince, a young bit-part actor who without warning stabbed the 50-year-old to death.

Coming out of the blue in this way and with Terriss a recognised name in the theatre world, the murder caused a sensation. Terriss was dead within minutes – he had been stabbed three times – his assailant had already been already seized by passers-by when the police arrived. Prince was quick to confess, telling officers, 'He has had due warning, and if he is dead, he knew what to expect from me.'

It transpired that Prince, twenty years his victim's junior, was well known to Terriss who had made repeated attempts to further his career. On a number of occasions he had managed to get the younger man small parts in shows in which he took the leading role, but Prince's drinking and occasionally erratic behaviour meant that this was becoming harder to do.

With Prince growing increasingly resentful and jealous of Terriss, things reached a head in early December when his former mentor was forced to arrange for him to be dismissed. On 13 December, Prince was asked in no uncertain terms to leave the Vaudeville Theatre and shortly afterwards the two men were heard arguing in a dressing room at the Adelphi.

Possibly the row was over money, as Terriss had previously negotiated for Prince to receive some help from the Actors' Benevolent Fund in nearby Adam Street. For some reason, the money was not forthcoming that day and, concluding that Terriss was to blame for this latest slight, Prince had hastened across the Strand to the Adelphi.

In so far as it was a premeditated attack, Prince might have been expected to hang, but following his arrest it was quickly determined that – besides being jealous of Terriss and convinced that he deserved much better roles than he was being offered – Prince was, in fact, insane. With no real case to answer, he was quietly committed to the Criminal Lunatic Asylum at Broadmoor, the apparent leniency of his punishment infuriating theatregoers and actors alike, who were not to know that he would stay locked up there until his death in 1937, aged 71.

The Actors' Benevolent Fund still survives, and today its own website refers to the case, suggesting that during his long incarceration Prince 'spent the rest of his days producing plays with himself as the leading character and the other inmates in supporting roles'. Terriss, meanwhile, continues to captivate audiences of a different kind, if not at Covent Garden then at the Adelphi where his ghost is also said occasionally still to tread the boards. A plaque at the rear records his murder.

LOUIS VOISIN AND BERTHE ROCHE

101 Charlotte Street, W1 (1917)
50 Munster Square, NW1 (1917)

'Blodie Belgiam'

On 2 November 1917, a road sweeper working his early morning beat in Regent Square, St Pancras came upon a package that had been thrown over the railings into the private central garden. Unwrapping an outer layer of what looked like sacking, he discovered a female trunk and arms. The police were called and shortly afterwards found the victim's legs in another parcel elsewhere in the square.

There was no sign of the head or hands, but while the victim's identity was yet to be established there were plenty of clues. Lettering on the hessian sack read 'Argentina La Plata Cold Storage' – a reference to a meat packing plant – with one parcel also containing a bedsheet with a clearly identifiable laundry mark, scraps of muslin, some ladies' underwear and a piece of paper bearing the legend 'blodie Belgiam'.

The laundry mark led the police straight to the home of a 32-year-old Frenchwoman called Emilienne Gerard who had not been seen for three days. In her rooms at No. 50 Munster Square they found a few small bloodstains, an IOU for £50 signed 'Louis Voisin' and a picture of a stocky, powerfully built man who was assumed to be Monsieur Voisin.

Quickly traced to his basement flat in Charlotte Street, Voisin turned out to be another French expat who was working as a butcher. This last observation was particularly interesting as an examination of the remains in Regent Square suggested the dismembering was the work of an expert, also muslin was at this time commonly used by butchers to wrap joints of meat. Voisin soon found himself at Bow Street helping the police with their enquiries, as was his companion, Berthe Roche.

From the start the evidence against him was compelling. He knew and had visited Madame Gerard on numerous occasions, he had a key to Munster Square and was paying her rent. When asked in the interview to write out 'bloody Belgium' – a clumsy ruse, presumably intended to throw police off the scent – he made the same spelling mistakes five times in succession. He also had a key to the coal cellar beneath the pavement outside No. 101 in which police found a barrel containing Madame Gerard's hands and head. Finally, a more detailed search of his own property uncovered several more bloodstains and a single earring.

A Home Office pathologist's report, prepared by the eminent Sir Bernard Spilsbury, revealed that Madame Gerard had been struck in the head and face a minimum of eight times and then been strangled while a towel had been held over her mouth to stifle her cries. It is assumed the earring had been lost during this struggle, which had clearly taken place at Charlotte Street rather than Munster Square.

It did not take long for the truth to emerge. The victim had ducked into her friend Voisin's basement to shelter from an air raid on the last night of October. She found him in the company of Roche. The two women quickly came to blows, at which point Madame Gerard had been hit repeatedly with a poker. It was Sir Bernard's opinion that this improvised weapon must have been wielded by Roche rather than Voisin who, being stronger, would almost certainly have killed her outright.

Voisin, however, had probably been responsible for silencing the victim with the towel and possibly had strangled her. Certainly, he was responsible for the skilled dissection, the disposal of the body – which had been stored briefly at Munster Square, hence the traces of blood there – and for the chillingly inept attempt at disguising the killing as a racist attack made at a time when Britain was at war.

With such a strong connection between perpetrator and victim, a clear motive, forensic evidence carelessly left all over the place, and body parts liberally scattered around central London, it is hard to believe that either Roche or Voisin could have imagined for a moment that they might get away with their crime. That said, in a sense the former did.

Bertha Roche was charged only as an accessory after the fact and received a sentence of seven years, of which she served just one and a half before going insane and dying of natural causes. Voisin, however, was to feel the full weight of the law and on 2 March the following year dropped through the hatch at Pentonville and was pronounced dead at the age of 42.

Unfortunately, all three addresses have now disappeared. The whole of Munster and most of Regent Square underwent complete redevelopment after being largely destroyed in the Blitz, while the butcher's address in Charlotte Street is now just a scruffy, litter-strewn service entrance to a residential block attached to University College, London.

MARGUERITE LAURENT FAHMI

Savoy Hotel, Strand, WC2 (1923)

'Qu'est-ce Que J'ai Fait, Mon Cher?'

The press love a good murder, and rarely more so than when an aristocrat is involved. In recent years, the disappearance of the 10th Earl of Shaftesbury in 2004 had all the makings of a perfect, if tragic, tabloid whodunnit, particularly when a body was discovered hidden in the French Alps and all the evidence pointed to his own wife, an exotically named former nightclub hostess.

In 1923, however, a similarly juicy story had emerged much closer to home with the protagonists giving it a hint of mysterious eastern glamour, although the action was set against the backdrop of London's Savoy Hotel. It was outside a suite in this celebrated hotel that the body of Ali Kamel Fahmi Bey was found shot to death.

This fabulously rich Egyptian princeling (one of the wealthiest, newspaper readers were breathlessly reminded) had married a Frenchwoman, Marguerite, who, after confessing to having shot the prince, found herself at Bow Street Magistrates' Court. Once there, Madame Fahmi's fabulous diamonds and emeralds attracted just as much comment as the details of her late husband's demise in the early hours of 10 July.

The case is most noteworthy, however, for her surprise acquittal. Madame Fahmi had never troubled to deny she had a gun in the hotel, nor that she had fired it at her husband. She nevertheless escaped a conviction even for manslaughter after what has been described as a truly bravura performance by her barrister, Sir Edward Marshall Hall, who had shrewdly gauged that his client's best chance lay an open appeal to the jury's solidly racist instincts.

The couple had married just eight months earlier. Marguerite was something of a gold-digger who must have considered the handsome 22-year-old Egyptian quite a catch. Strictly speaking, Fahmi was a nobleman rather than a prince, but when travelling abroad neither of them troubled to put anyone right when they were mistakenly introduced as prince and princess.

Theirs was evidently something of a fiery relationship, and witnesses spoke of seeing Ali's scratched face and bruising showing through Marguerite's make-up. Shortly after checking into the Savoy on this occasion, Marguerite had summoned the hotel doctor and showed him some minor injuries, which she blamed on her husband's preference for what she described as 'unnatural intercourse'. Perhaps already thinking of divorce, she had requested some kind of certificate relating to her condition.

On 9 July, the couple went to the theatre – as it happens, to see *The Merry Widow* – and afterwards were observed arguing loudly in the hotel dining room. With each threatening the other with a beating from an empty wine bottle, they were eventually pacified by the maître d' and Madame Fahmi went alone up to bed after briefly taking in the house band in the ballroom.

At 2 a.m. the following morning three shots were heard. The night porter later related how he had found Ali bleeding heavily from a head wound and his wife, having dropped a black hand-gun, saying over and over, '*Qu'est-ce que j'ai fait, mon cher?*' ('What have I done, my dear?').

In court the following September, Sir Edward Marshall Hall lost no opportunity in portraying the victim as a violent and immoral alien; a sinister foreigner with 'abnormal tendencies' who, as likely as not, was engaged in a gross and illegal relationship with his male secretary. He was an Oriental, given to a life of debauchery and 'obsessed with his sexual prowess', said Sir Edward. Ali's crime was to look on his wife as merely another possession to be used and abused at will.

Thereafter, the proceedings were never anything but unbalanced in her favour, with the judge on the one hand allowing a description of the potentate's household as a conspiracy of 'numerous ugly, black, half-civilised manservants', and on the other refusing permission for the prosecution even to cross-examine Madame Fahmi.

In the end, it was left to Sir Edward to deal the final blow, observing that while 'we in this country put our women on a pedestal, in Egypt they have not the same views'. Addressing the all-white jury, he implored them 'to open the gate and let this white woman go back into the light of God's great western sun'. To the undisguised fury of the Egyptian Ambassador in London, the jury agreed, allowing Madame Fahmi to leave the court a free woman.

Press opinion across the Middle East was outraged, the venerable *Al-Ahram* newspaper fuming at descriptions of Egypt's 'backwardness' and 'barbarity'. Closer to home, a very different picture of Madame Fahmi soon emerged, describing her earlier career as a prostitute and a 15-year-old unmarried mother. Such as it was, her reputation never recovered, and when she was unable to inherit her husband's reputed £2 million fortune she found herself a laughing stock when she returned home to Paris. She died more or less a recluse at the age of 81 in January 1971.

JOHN ROBINSON

Charing Cross Station, Strand, WC2 (1927)
86 Rochester Row, SW1 (1927)

'1 Want to Tell You all About it. I Done it and Cut Her Up.'

The name Robinson may be all but forgotten and the precise details of his crime a little hazy, but the phrase 'Charing Cross Trunk Murder' still presses all the right buttons to rank alongside Rillington Place or the Ratcliffe Highway.

On 6 May 1927, after leaving a substantial black trunk and very specific instructions as to its handling, a man walked out of the left luggage office at Charing Cross Station and climbed into a cab before disappearing along the Strand. The staff probably thought no more about it until a few days later when a dreadful smell was traced to the trunk and the police were called.

With a sense of foreboding, the police opened the trunk on 10 May, revealing a dismembered corpse with each of the limbs individually wrapped in brown paper. An examination of the remains, once again by Sir Bernard Spilsbury, determined that the body was that of a woman: she was stocky, about 35 years old, and had bruising to the stomach, back and forehead which had been inflicted while she was unconscious.

The address on the trunk drew a blank but, not for the first time, a laundry mark provided a useful clue, suggesting the corpse belonged to a 'Mrs Roles'. For a short while, a Mrs Roles had been employed as a cook at a private address in Chelsea, and she seemed to answer Sir Bernard's description.

Investigations continued, and after an appeal was published in the London dailies, a shop owner in Brixton supplied the police with a description of a moustachioed man in his mid-thirties who had bought just such a trunk. At the same time, a cab driver came forward saying he had helped load a trunk into his cab for transfer to Charing Cross. His description of his fare sounded remarkably similar to that provided by the shop owner.

The cabbie's pick-up had been at No. 86 Rochester Row near Victoria, where police found the hastily vacated but scrupulously clean – suspiciously clean, even – office of 35-year-old estate agent John Robinson. He had not been seen by his fellow tenants since 6 May but was soon tracked down to an address in De Laune Street, Kennington and was taken to Scotland Yard for questioning.

Initially, Robinson denied all knowledge of the crime and neither the shopkeeper nor the cab driver were able to pick him out in an identity parade, although with his neat turnout and military bearing the reality was very close to their recollections. Robinson was therefore released and only later changed his story when another, more careful search of the third-floor premises turned up a matchstick in the bin on which was a tiny trace of blood.

Officers now thought that having killed and dismembered his victim, the murderer had painstakingly cleaned the office to get rid of the evidence but then carelessly discarded the match after sitting back to enjoy a well-earned cigarette. Robinson was rearrested, and this time decided he may as well spill the beans. 'I want to tell you all about it,' he told the detective who interviewed him, 'I done it and cut her up.'

'Mrs Roles' turned out to be Minnie Bonati, the former wife of an Italian waiter, who was in the habit of supplementing her work as a domestic servant with a little part-time prostitution. Robinson said she had approached him outside Victoria Station, either to beg for money or more likely to pick up some business, and the two had returned to his rented office at No. 86. A quarrel took place, presumably about the money, during which she had been suffocated by his attempts to quieten her down.

It is tempting to suppose that had he crossed the road to Rochester Road Police Station at this point and explained what had happened, Robinson might have escaped with a charge of manslaughter. This would be on the grounds that – were his story true – the death would appear to have been accidental. Instead, he panicked at the sight of what he had done and returned to the street, where he bought a large kitchen knife which he then used to dismember the corpse. Bonati's constituent parts were then packed into a cheap, 12-shilling trunk, which he deposited at the railway left luggage office.

Robinson's late confession and the very considered efforts he went to in order to conceal his crime left him little room for manoeuvre at his trial on 11 July at the Old Bailey. Witnesses testified that the victim was a violent alcoholic, but it took the jury less than an hour to find John Robinson guilty of killing her and he was hanged at Pentonville on 12 August.

The office at No. 86 disappeared long ago, but the row of shops opposite the brown brick office block that now occupies the site gives a good impression of how it would have looked in the 1920s.

ALEC DE ANTIQUIS

73–75 Charlotte Street, W1 (1947)
Charlotte Street/Tottenham Street junction, W1 (1947)

'A Dead Man Lies on a London Pavement'

The cold-blooded murder of motorcycle mechanic and father of six Alec de Antiquis in broad daylight on a West End street created a wave of fear across the capital. It is popularly supposed to have been witnessed by hangman Albert Pierrepoint as he enjoyed a drink at the Fitzroy Tavern.

At the time, speculation was rife that gun crime and gang violence were getting out of hand, perhaps the only surprise being that the incident took place in 1947 rather than the present day. Shortly after 2.30 p.m. on 29 April, the 31-year-old had been gunned down as he attempted to waylay three armed robbers making their escape after visiting the premises of Jay's Jewellers on Charlotte Street in Fitzrovia. The gang managed successfully to disappear into the crowds when their black Vauxhall's escape route was blocked by traffic, and immediately became the target of one of the largest manhunts London had yet seen.

Violent crime in the capital was experiencing something of a peak in the immediate post-war period, in part, it has been argued, because a flood of handguns had come onto the market at the close of hostilities. Droves of former servicemen who were now unemployed had turned to crime after being demobbed, and a whole generation of poorly educated delinquents had grown up while their fathers were away fighting.

A recent weapons amnesty had succeeded in taking more than 18,000 illegally held guns out of circulation on a single day but, with possession of a weapon sometimes attracting fines of only a couple of pounds or less, armed attacks in central London were still very much on the rise.

Against this background, the death of the Anglo-Italian de Antiquis must have been a gift to the press, his story one of an innocent bystander attempting to prevent a crime, and a young husband and father standing up for justice against a criminal element which seemed to be getting the upper hand. In just such a vein, one newspaper described how his red motorcycle had been abandoned at the junction with Tottenham Street and 'a dead man lies on a London pavement ... a sight we associate with Chicago but not with the capital of Britain'. Others editorialised about the unwelcome influence of the latest wave of mobster films from Hollywood and the lenient punishments being handed out by the courts to anyone who sought to emulate this new class of American anti-hero.

Scotland Yard responded by putting one of its best men on the case. Chief Inspector Robert Fabian quickly tracked down his three suspects using a combination of painstaking forensic examination and careful referencing and cross-referencing of the huge mass of information he and his men had gathered during the murder investigation. Before long, a gun was recovered from the muddy shore of the Thames and, while witness statements often proved contradictory, a taxi driver recalled seeing two men running into a building on Tottenham Court Road. At Brook House police found a discarded raincoat belonging to Charles Henry Jenkins, a 23-year-old with definite 'form'.

The arrest of two of his associates quickly followed, both of them – Christopher James Geraghty (aged 21) and Terence Peter Rolt (aged 17) – accusing the older man at the first chance they got. All three found themselves in the dock on 21 July charged with murder, and within a week all three had been found guilty.

Being of age, Jenkins and Geraghty were sentenced to death and were hanged side by side at Pentonville Prison on 19 September 1947. Rolt escaped a similar fate, however, and being under 18 at the time was instead detained at Her Majesty's pleasure before being released on licence after serving nine and a half years.

The jeweller's is long gone and the location is now a contraception clinic. More than sixty years later, the case has been more or less forgotten, along with the names of the murderers and their victim. Their story cast a long shadow, however, providing the inspiration for an Ealing Studio production called *The Blue Lamp*, which opened two years later. In it, a gunman (played by Dirk Bogarde) fleeing the scene of a crime shoots dead a policeman who is attempting to arrest him.

The film, in a very real sense, set the template for the fictional 'British bobby' for many years to come. Its spin-offs included not one but two new television dramas: *Fabian of the Yard* and the even more successful *Dixon of Dock Green*, which saw the murdered policeman restored to health and the comforting authority figure of Jack Warner on our screens for the next twenty-one years.

EDWIN BUSH

23 Cecil Court, WC2 (1961)

'Speaking Personally, the World is Better Off Without Me'

Cecil Court has long been a mecca for bibliophiles as well as a useful shortcut for non-readers making their way west on foot from St Martin's Lane. It was briefly home to the young Mozart and his family in 1764, and the location of the first Foyles Bookshop before it moved to much larger premises in Charing Cross Road.

On 3 March 1961, it hit the headlines when an assistant at Louis Meier's antique shop was discovered brutally murdered at the back of the premises. Mrs Elsie May Batten (59) had multiple stab wounds, from two of which protruded the ivory handles of a pair of antique daggers.

Mrs Batten's employer had not been present at the time of the attack, but on discovering the body he immediately called the police. Later that day, the victim was identified by her husband, Mark Batten, a distinguished sculptor and former associate of Eric Gill, whose statue *Diogenist* can still be seen in Golders Hill Park, NW11.

When questioned by detectives, the shop owner recalled a visit the previous day by a young man of mixed race who had expressed an interest in a curved dress sword and two antique daggers. He left without buying anything, but the sword was now missing and of course the antique daggers were now important pieces of evidence.

Elsie Batten's killer was to become the first murderer in Britain to be apprehended using an 'identikit' image. From Mr Meier's recollections, Bow Street Station's Detective Sergeant Raymond Dagg was able to produce a hand-drawn identikit likeness of the mysterious visitor using a system newly arrived from North America. Dagg also interviewed neighbouring shop owners, one of whom said he had been approached by a young man, possibly Indian, who had attempted to sell him a sword for £15. He provided a description from which the police officer was able to draft a second identikit image. The similarity between the two drawings was striking, and posters were produced showing the two images side by side and circulated to police stations within the capital and the press.

Just five days after the murder, a policeman on duty in Old Compton Street had a lucky break. PC Arthur Cole of West End Central collared a man who closely matched the descriptions given by Meier and his Cecil Court neighbour. The man was taken into custody with his girlfriend. Edwin Bush (aged 21) agreed that the identikit pictures bore a certain likeness but denied that he had any connection with Cecil Court or the late Mrs Batten. When interviewed on the evening of 8 March by two senior officers, he said he had an alibi for the day in question, but when this could not be substantiated, he was put into an identity parade. Louis Meier proved unable to identify him, but Paul Roberts picked him out and confirmed that Bush was the young man who had offered to sell him the sword for £15.

At this point, Bush agreed to co-operate and thereafter provided a full statement while insisting that his girlfriend had played no part whatsoever in the robbery or murder. He had, he said, been intending to steal the sword but had lost his nerve, picked up a stone vase and hit Mrs Batten. 'I don't know what came over me. Speaking personally, the world is better off without me.'

Ahead of his trial, background checks revealed an all too familiar picture. The defendant's living conditions when he was a child had been sufficiently poor as to warrant an investigation by the National Society for the Prevention of Cruelty to Children (NSPCC) and subsequently he had spent a period in a children's home and several spells in borstal for housebreaking and theft.

This latest crime was particularly brutal and wholly unprovoked, however, and when committed to trial at the Old Bailey on 10 May 1961, the verdict must have seemed almost a formality. So, too, the sentence, since the murder of Mrs Batten in Cecil Court had been committed in the 'course or furtherance of theft', a capital offence specifically referenced in the 1957 Homicide Act. Once underway, the proceedings took less than two days to complete and, after being sentenced to death, Bush was hanged at Pentonville on 6 July.

The shop still exists as a bookseller's, and having played such an historic and pioneering role in murder detection, the two identikit images were lodged in the National Archives, under the catalogue reference CRIM 1/3661.

5

KENSINGTON AND CHELSEA

WALTER MILLER

24 Wellington Square, SW3 (1870)
15 Paultons Square, SW3 (1870)

'You Make Your Charge and I Will Pay'

A matched pair of violent, unprovoked and readily solved crimes – that the press quickly tagged as the 'Chelsea Murders' – were committed by a handyman with such an obvious connection to the victims that one struggles to imagine how he could have expected to get away with it.

The handyman was Walter Miller, a Scotsman, aged 31. On 9 May 1870 he was working for 84-year-old Elias Huelin, a largely retired clergyman who was an occasional assistant chaplain at nearby Brompton Cemetery. In particular, Miller was required to finish some plastering at a property in Wellington Square.

On calling at the house that morning to see how the work was progressing, the Reverend Huelin was hit over the head with a spade and crammed into a cupboard after being searched and relieved of any valuables. Huelin, an expat French Protestant, had owned the house together with another slightly smaller one in Paultons Square, a few minutes' walk away.

Having concealed his body in a hasty fashion, Miller set off down the King's Road, apparently determined to surprise the clergyman's housekeeper and do away with her as well. At the second address, he found the woman in question, Mrs Ann Boss, who he strangled with a length of rope before hiding her away in a large wooden box.

In so far as he had a plan, Miller had apparently hoped to rob the houses of anything he could turn into cash. He then passed himself off as Huelin's nephew – newly arrived from Jersey and sporting an obviously dyed beard – to somehow secure legal title to the two valuable properties and any others Huelin had in the vicinity.

Before he could put this final stage into operation, however, Miller felt he had earned a drink – possibly a fair few of them, in fact – and to this end he spent much of the following day taking cabs from one tavern to the next. Buying drinks for anyone who wanted one and affecting a very poor and declining imitation of what he assumed to be a French accent, Miller had soon managed quite effectively to draw attention to himself at a time when a smarter man might have gone to ground.

While he did not know it yet, there were already concerns about the old French gentleman: one witness in the King's Road, having seen his old friend step off an omnibus and go into the square, was wondering how it was he had not seen him emerge. At the same time, Miller had asked a workman to go around to the elegant Wellington Square house in order to lift a drain, even though the owner was clearly nowhere to be seen when he got there.

Miller's next mistake was to ask a local greengrocer, Henry Piper, if he could use his cart to move some effects out of the other house. When Piper got to Paultons Square and asked how much he was to be paid for doing this, Miller answered somewhat strangely, 'Me pay you anything you charge, you make your charge and I will pay.'

Among the things to be moved was the large wooden box containing Mrs Boss, which had been firmly strapped shut.

Unfortunately, on lifting it, Piper felt a damp sensation on his hands and realised that it was covered with fresh blood, which had also pooled on the floor below.

When he questioned Miller about this, the latter's accent slipped and, thinking quickly, Piper manoeuvred him up the basement stairs and out into the square. By now it was raining hard and Miller was able to break free. As he made a run for it, Piper alerted a police constable who was sheltering under a lamp and the Scotsman was very soon under arrest.

While he was being manhandled to the police station, a sergeant returned to the house with Piper and, using a fire poker, broke open the chest to find the remains of Mrs Boss with a length of clothes line still knotted around her throat. Shortly afterwards, a thorough search of the Wellington Square house revealed the body of Reverend Huelin which had been taken from the cupboard and pushed down into the newly excavated drain.

After being formally arrested, Miller took poison which had apparently been procured at a local chemist on the afternoon of the second murder, almost in anticipation that such an ill-conceived plan was bound to fail. But, after a short stay in St George's Hospital – now remodelled as the Lanesborough Hotel – the presumed double murderer was considered fit enough to plead and his trial was scheduled to be heard at the Old Bailey on 11 July.

Briefly, Miller made an attempt to blame the double killing on the nephew he had impersonated, but when this failed, he was sentenced to death by a judge who also ordered a payment of £50 to be made to Henry Piper for his quick thinking and courage.

ERNEST OLDHAM

31 Pembroke Gardens, W8 (1933)

'Completely in the Hands of the OGPU'

The first of a number of espionage-related deaths in the royal borough, Ernest Holloway Oldham seemed to be an otherwise unimportant, middle-ranking civil servant. However, he was secretly in the employ of OGPU – Stalin's secret police, a forerunner of the KGB – and is now known to have spied against Britain in the 1920s and early 1930s.

A mercenary volunteer to the Communist cause rather than an ideological recruit from the colleges at Cambridge, Oldham worked as a cipher clerk at the Foreign Office. He was an alcoholic and prolific drug user. He ran into money problems shortly after his marriage in 1927 but seemed, nevertheless, to be able to maintain an attractive detached house in a smart part of town where he employed a uniformed chauffeur.

Colleagues at the Foreign Office perhaps assumed he had a private income, but the truth was somewhat darker. On a trip to Paris in late 1927 or early 1928, Oldham had presented himself at the Russian Embassy, calling himself 'Mr Scott', and offered his services. Unsurprisingly perhaps, the offer was rejected. The Soviets were confident that such a straightforward approach could be nothing but a particularly clumsy and amateurish effort at infiltration by the British security services.

Undeterred, Oldham made a second visit, this time receiving a more cordial welcome having, in the meantime, been able to demonstrate the value of the information that passed through his hands back in London. Still no agreement was reached, however, but a few months later an agent known as 'Galleni' was despatched to London with instructions to locate and recruit the mysterious Mr Scott.

Incredibly, Galleni asked the Metropolitan Police to help track his man down, claiming to have been involved in a minor car accident in Paris with an unnamed British civil servant and providing the date. The police helpfully supplied the home addresses of several Foreign Office officials who were known to have been in the French capital at the time. Setting out to find his man, Galleni soon struck gold in Pembroke Gardens.

Galleni reportedly handed Oldham £2,000 in cash and a relationship was quickly established, only for it to hit the buffers soon afterwards as Oldham's drinking got more and more out of hand. In 1932, he lost his job after being caught drunk once too often; a potentially catastrophic development which left him (in the words of an official MI5 file later produced on the case) 'completely in the hands of the OGPU'.

The same file goes on to note how, now in desperate straits financially, Oldham 'continued to obtain Foreign Office material by making use of his previous position there'. It seems that, despite being sacked for drunkenness, security in Whitehall was so slack that a former employee was somehow still permitted to visit his old office to converse with old colleagues, and even to store personal items in the 'confidential presses' or office safe.

His controller at OGPU must have been amazed when he heard this, and presumably would have kept paying Oldham for as long as useful snippets of intelligence continued to flow from London to Paris via Galleni. But unfortunately, Oldham's days were numbered. His addiction to drugs and alcohol dramatically reduced his usefulness to the Soviets and repeatedly tried Galleni's patience. At one point, the latter even threatened to expose his own agent to MI5 unless Oldham shaped up and got a grip.

In fact, by this stage the hapless Oldham may well have been unable to help himself. The same MI5 files suggest he was having some kind of breakdown. They describe how, on one occasion while meeting his Soviet handler in the dark obscurity of a cinema, Oldham caused a scene because Galleni neglected to get to his feet when 'God Save the King' was played.

A few weeks after this, Oldham was suspected of making copies of the cipher room keys when a set was returned to Whitehall with traces of wax or soap still clearly visible. It seems incredible that he would have had an opportunity to do this, but at last his superiors began to sit up and take notice. MI5 was called in to put Oldham under surveillance.

A few days later, he was found dead in the flat at Pembroke Gardens, wearing night attire and with his head in the oven.

Officially, the death was described as a suicide, a case of a man who had no desire to face his creditors, or maybe who took the obvious way out after realising that MI5 was onto him and that he might hang. But just as likely, the MI5 file admits, is that, having outlived his usefulness, Oldham was bumped off by Stalin's agents who were sensibly covering their tracks.

JOHN HAIGH

79 Gloucester Road, SW7 (1949)
The Goat, 3 Kensington High Street, W8 (1944)

'What Are the Chances of Anyone Getting Out of Broadmoor?'

As a serial killer who the popular press gleefully branded the 'Kensington Vampire', the grisly reputation of the short but dapper John Haigh depends less on his confession (that he drank the blood of his victims) than on the means by which he chose to conceal his crimes. In 1949, the so-called Acid Bath Murderer was hanged at Wandsworth, and it is by this name that he has remained foremost in the public's imagination.

In fact, it seems quite unlikely that the vampire claim was anything more than a desperate bid by Haigh to feign insanity and escape the noose. Otherwise, he made little attempt to help himself after his arrest, even going so far as to suggest that he had killed nine people rather than the one for which he first came under suspicion. Now it seems that the precise extent of his crimes will probably never be known, as he rid himself of the bodies by dissolving them in drums of concentrated prussic acid and disposing of the residue by pouring it down a drain.

As a small-scale manufacturer of false fingernails, the former Wakefield Cathedral chorister had access to the necessary quantities of acid, which he kept in a basement workshop beneath what is now a language school and a neighbouring Kentucky

Fried Chicken in Gloucester Road. Also known as hydrogen cyanide, prussic acid is highly toxic and extremely corrosive, something Haigh demonstrated to his own satisfaction by dissolving several mice in it after conceiving his plan while in prison on a charge of fraud.

His first victim was William Donald McSwann, an acquaintance he bumped into by chance at The Goat in Kensington High Street. Inviting McSwann back to his basement on 6 September 1944, Haigh knocked him unconscious, doubtless taking some pleasure in the successful prosecution of a carefully thought out scheme although his motivation was also partly mercenary.

Having met McSwann's parents, he knew them to be well off. He also knew they would probably try and enlist his help in locating their missing son, and ten months later they too found their way to the basement, where they were despatched in a similarly brutal manner. Forging documents that appeared to give him power of attorney over their estate, Haigh moved into the nearby Onslow Court Hotel. There, clearing around £4,000 by selling various McSwann properties, he set himself up as a respectable businessman about town.

It was at Onslow Court – now Jury's Kensington Hotel – that Haigh befriended Olivia Durand-Deacon, a wealthy widow, aged 69. Having managed to interest her in the technicalities of artificial nail production, Haigh invited her to a second workshop he had rented at Leopold Road, Crawley. After killing her there, dismembering the body and setting it to dissolve in another 40-gallon container of acid, Haigh returned to London with her jewellery which, again, he sold.

Unfortunately for Haigh, the widow may have been lonely, but she was not without friends and her sudden and unexplained disappearance led another hotel resident, Constance

Lane, to take her suspicions to the police. Acting on a hunch, one of the detectives did a bit of digging around and discovered in pretty short order that Haigh had convictions for fraud, selling stolen cars and looting bombed-out buildings. He was also in arrears at the hotel, suggesting he had money troubles.

When pulled in for questioning, Haigh at first refused to co-operate but then surprised one of the investigating officers by asking, 'What are the chances of anyone getting out of Broadmoor?' Shortly afterwards, Haigh appeared to confess but, apparently believing there could be no court case or conviction without a body, he seemed to think he might have got away with it.

Unfortunately for him, he had reckoned without the determination of Detective Inspector Shelley-Symes, and the tenacity of the Home Office pathologist, Dr Keith Simpson. Simpson's painstaking examination of the two workshops soon uncovered more than 28lb of a suspiciously greasy substance (later identified as human fat), three gallstones, a readily identifiable set of female dentures and eighteen fragments of human bone.

Haigh's trial lasted just two days and saw him charged with only one murder, although he confessed to eight more, including a Dr Henderson and his wife, a woman from Hammersmith and another he said he had met at Eastbourne. His lawyers argued forcefully that he was insane and pointed to a traumatic childhood during which he had been bullied by his fanatically strict Plymouth Brethren parents.

For his part, Haigh displayed what a medical witness described as a 'callous, cheerful, bland and almost friendly indifference', and the jury remained unpersuaded. Come the second day, they took just seventeen minutes to convict.

On the bright, sunny morning of 10 August 1949, London's Acid Bath Murderer was hanged by the neck until he was dead.

CHRISTINE GRANVILLE

Shellbourne Hotel, 1 Lexham Gardens, W8 (1952)

'To Kill is the Final Possession'

A beautiful and accomplished wartime agent, who provided the model for at least two Bond girls – 'Vesper Lynd' and 'Tatiana Romanova' – Krystyna Skarbek was the daughter of a Polish count and distantly related to the composer Chopin. She was recruited into Britain's Special Operations Executive (SOE) in 1940 and adopted the name Christine Granville as her *nom de guerre*. She decided to keep it when she settled in London after the war.

Her skills as a spy are well documented, and it has been suggested that it was her success in the role which helped persuade the authorities that SOE might profit by recruiting more women for espionage and sabotage work in occupied Europe. She was exceptionally resourceful, and once escaped from the Gestapo after faking the symptoms of tuberculosis by biting her tongue until it bled. In July 1944 she was parachuted into France, where she assisted a joint force of Italian partisans and the French Maquis in harrying the Germans in the Alps.

Granville was also credited with saving the lives of several SOE colleagues by successfully bribing the officer who proposed shooting them and persuading him that, as the niece of General

Montgomery, she would ensure that he was targeted for special retribution after the war. Of course, she was no such thing, and only later realised quite how much danger she had put herself in, asking, 'What have I done? They could have shot me as well.'

For these and other exploits she was awarded the George Medal and the French *Croix de Guerre*, subsequently catching the eye of the author and Naval Intelligence operative Ian Fleming. He incorporated elements of her glamorous personality into two characters in his books, *Casino Royale* and *From Russia With Love.*

When the war ended, however, Granville found herself with no country to return to. With no reserves to fall back on she was forced to find work to support herself financially. At various times, she was employed as a housekeeper in a hotel, a telephone switchboard operator at India House on Aldwych, and a shop assistant at Harrods. Eventually, she applied for a more suitable-sounding post with the British United Nations Mission in Geneva, but her application was turned down because she was not British born.

In desperation, in 1951 Granville applied for another rather menial post, as a stewardess on the liner *Winchester Castle* and then the *Rauhine*, which was bound for Australia. Unfortunately, en route she is said to have upset members of the crew by wearing her medals, although this was by no means her own choice, but something insisted upon by the captain. Observing what was going on, an Irish cabin attendant called Dennis Muldowney sprang to her defence, but then mistook her expression of thanks for an expression of interest and started stalking her once they returned to England.

On 15 June 1952, the 44-year-old checked into her hotel in Lexham Gardens and was confronted by Muldowney, who questioned her about a trip she was planning to see a former lover and SOE comrade, the one-legged Polish war hero Andrzej Kowerski. As he became increasingly agitated on hearing her plans, Muldowney produced a knife.

The hotel's night porter later described how he had run to Granville's aid after hearing her shout, 'Get him off me!' By the time he reached the source of the commotion, Granville was already dead from a chest wound. Muldowney freely admitted that he had killed her and waited quietly while the police were summoned. When the officers arrived, he confessed to the crime, telling them angrily, 'I built all my dreams around her, but she was playing me for a fool.'

Muldowney stuck by this version of events in his trial at the Old Bailey and insisted, 'To kill is the final possession.' As a result of such claims and a guilty plea, his murder trial was to be one of the shortest on record – a mere three minutes from start to finish.

Muldowney went to Pentonville Prison and was hanged on 30 September 1952, with the press describing his victim as 'the modern pimpernel no man could resist'. To them and to the public, Granville's story also proved irresistible, even without the 007 connection and, at the time of writing, newspapers in Britain and Poland were abuzz with talk of a new movie, linking Eva Green – Vesper Lynd in the remake of *Casino Royale* – with the lead role in a film of Granville's life.

KENNETH GILBERT AND IAN GRANT

Aban Court Hotel, 25 Harrington Gardens, SW7
(1954)

Good Friends to the End

Whether it is better to be hanged alone or in the company of a good friend is happily one of life's imponderables, although to most the thought of two men being hanged side by side is even more chilling than the two of them being despatched out of sight of each other. Even so, for a long time double hangings of this sort were considered acceptable for partners in crime, and the practice was not outlawed in this country until the Homicide Act of 1957. The Act determined that in cases in which more than one person was to be hanged for the same offence, the prisoners would be executed simultaneously but at different prisons, and as a result of this ruling Gilbert and Grant are today remembered as the last two to receive their punishment in the old-fashioned manner.

Their brutally clumsy handiwork was first observed by kitchen staff at Aban Court Hotel in South Kensington, who arrived for work on the morning of 9 March 1954 to find the body of a colleague, George Smart, bound, gagged and stuffed in the servery. Despite a considerable head injury, the 55-year-old night porter had struggled to free himself, managed to release his arms but then suffocated on the gag.

Robbery appeared to be the motive rather than straight-forward murder, although when the police were called it was discovered that only £2 was missing from the cash register in the hotel bar, together with a few packs of cigarettes. Put like that, it was hardly the crime of the century, nor were those responsible for the theft at all impressive in the way they had gone about committing or concealing the crime.

Consequently, it took the police barely a day to get both Gilbert and Grant into custody. Both were themselves hotel porters, and with Gilbert a former employee of the Aban Court, he was certain to come under suspicion sooner rather than later.

Grant did not help matters either, boasting to a work colleague that he had stolen some cigarettes from another hotel the night before and – even more bizarrely – admitting to having 'done a man in' when the evening papers ran a story about the discovery of Smart's body. When asked to collect the cigarettes from Grant's hiding place, the colleague decided to report him to the police instead and told them where the cigarettes could be found.

On being questioned about this, the pair naturally denied they had any intention of killing the night porter and both claimed to have been shocked to hear of his death. They confirmed they had attacked him, however, and 22-year-old Gilbert recalled landing 'a light blow to the stomach'. Grant, who was two years older, admitted he had punched Smart twice on the jaw. He had also stuffed a napkin into the victim's mouth while gagging him with a bandage although, like Gilbert, he attempted to shift the blame for the death onto his accomplice.

In court, the defence had hoped to secure a conviction for manslaughter, and in retrospect it does seem likely that – stupidly ill-conceived as the crime was – there was no intention beforehand to murder the older man for a couple of pounds and some smokes. But, summing up, Mr Justice Glyn-Jones made clear his opinion that the case was indeed one of murder, and he agreed with the prosecuting barrister. Even had they not intended to kill or cause serious harm, the fact that one or other of the two men might have contemplated violence to expedite a robbery was sufficient to make both men murderers.

Thus, in just twenty minutes were the fates of Gilbert and Grant sealed, the jury returning from their deliberations with verdicts of guilty for both men. The two immediately appealed against this judgement, but their appeals were quickly turned down by Lord Chief Justice of England and Wales, Lord Goddard, and the death sentences were allowed to stand.

Lord Goddard once famously dismissed six appeals in under an hour, and in all likelihood a different defence might have produced a different result. Even so, with each man intent on accusing the other, the end result was that both would hang. On 17 June 1954, Britain's last side-by-side execution was carried out at Pentonville Prison under the supervision of Albert Pierrepoint, with the help of Royston Rickard, Harry Smith and Joe Broadbent – three assistants instead of the usual one.

GUNTER PODOLA

105 Onslow Square, SW7 (1959)
95 Queen's Gate, SW7 (1959)

'It Wasn't Me, but Someone Who Looked Like Me'

A timely change in the law meant that Harry Roberts (see p. 213) was lucky enough to become the first convicted police killer to escape the noose. However, Gunter Fritz Erwin Podola had no such luck, and instead became the last man in Britain to be sent to the gallows for much the same crime.

Born in Berlin in 1929 and an enthusiastic member of the Hitler Youth, Podola arrived in London at the age of 30 having already spent time in Canada, where he had served two jail terms for theft and burglary. He was unskilled, unemployed and moving from one seedy Kensington hotel to another; within a couple of months he had come to the attention of the police following a burglary at an address in Roland Gardens.

The tip-off came from the victim, a Mrs Verne Schieffman, who said that Podola had attempted to blackmail her by claiming to have discovered something incriminating while burgling her flat. She knew he was lying, there was nothing in the flat to incriminate her, and knowing he would call back she alerted the police who began monitoring her telephone line.

On 13 July she received a call, which the police traced to a telephone box at South Kensington Underground Station. Two officers, Detective Sergeants Purdy and Sandford, were quickly in attendance and apprehended Podola on the spot. However, on the way to their vehicle Podola made a break a for it, running to a house at 105 Onslow Square and concealing himself behind a pillar in the hall. When Purdy (aged 43) entered the building he was shot dead and Podola escaped.

Three days later, with the police making enquiries all over the area, Podola was traced to another address at 95 Queen's Gate. Police broke into a room which had been identified as belonging to the gunman, and after some time emerged with their prisoner sporting a bruised face and a very obvious black eye. After a search of the premises, an automatic weapon was found concealed in the attic of the hotel.

At the time, it was said that his injuries came about when Podola was struck by his bedroom door as it was knocked off its hinges, although the strong suspicion at the time was that Purdy's colleagues might have had a hand in it. Either way, Podola seemed to be in shock and, after being taken to St Stephen's Hospital in the Fulham Road, he was said to be exhibiting the signs of someone suffering from amnesia.

On 18 July at the Central Criminal Court at the Old Bailey, the defence, led by Mr Frederick Lawton KC, attempted to demonstrate that a series of fainting fits and memory loss rendered their client unfit to plead. It was also argued that Podola's amnesia was the direct result of injuries sustained during his (second) arrest and he was unable to recall with any clarity the events of the previous few days. Unfortunately for Podola, the jury decided against this, and the trial was reset for the next day with the same judge, Mr Justice Edmund Davies, but a new jury.

In court on 19 July, Podola's brief stated that as he had been unable to obtain new instructions from his client, he would be unable to do anything more than test the evidence of the other side. To this end, he suggested that the killing was inadvertent and the gun might have been discharged accidentally while being entrusted to DS Purdy's care. This was denied by an expert from the Metropolitan Police Forensic Laboratory, and after thirty-five minutes the jury returned to the courtroom to pronounce Gunter Podola guilty of capital murder.

When he was sentenced to death the still silent Podola made no appeal, leaving it to the Home Secretary of the day, R.A. Butler, to refer the case on the grounds of his possible unfitness to plead. On 15 October, the Court of Criminal Appeal requested an examination to be made of Podola's mental state, after which a medical tribunal met to agree that his amnesia had almost certainly been faked. This judgement was verified shortly afterwards, with Podola suddenly 'remembering' that now he thought about it he had actually been busily engaged in burgling somewhere else at the time of the murder so it must have been committed by his double ...

On 20 October, however, the Court of Criminal Appeal was unpersuaded and found the trial of Gunter Podola to have been fair and just. Sixteen days later, he was hanged at Wandsworth and buried within the prison walls.

6

NORTH LONDON

FREDERICK HENRY SEDDON

63 Tollington Park, N4 (1911)

'It is Not for Me to Harrow Your Feelings'

Henry Seddon was a lapsed Freemason who laboured long hours to support his large family, or possibly just a greedy schemer for whom the acquisition of wealth trumped any and all moral considerations. Seddon was a superintendent of collectors for a large industrial insurance company and ran another business on the side selling second-hand clothes from a lock-up shop at No. 276 Seven Sisters Road.

By 1910, aged 40, he was also something of a small-time property speculator, buying and selling places whenever he could and renting out a four-room flat on the second floor of the family's large house in Upper Holloway to rake in a little more cash. His tenant that summer was the unfortunate Eliza Mary Barrow, a spinster nearly ten years his senior who had a reasonable investment portfolio of her own, the income from which she used to look after the orphaned son and daughter of a previous landlord.

Over a period of some months, Seddon managed to inveigle his way into the spinster's inner circle, manoeuvring himself into the position of her unpaid financial adviser while using the opportunity to extract whatever he could for himself. Before very long, he had offered to forego the rent and provide her with a modest annuity, in return for which she would transfer into his name £1,500 of India stock – or nearly 40 per cent of her net worth.

The following year, he raised her annuity to £3 a week, whereupon the lease on the Buck's Head pub in Camden High Street moved from her portfolio into his, along with an adjoining barber's shop. Shortly after this, he advised her to entrust to his care several hundred pounds from her savings account, a move he said would insulate her from the supposed long-term effects of Lloyd George's controversial 1909 budget.

In August, the Seddons – husband, wife, five children and an elderly father – took a break at Southend-on-Sea. Miss Barrow accompanied the family and brought with her the young boy who had been left in her care. However, on returning home she was suddenly taken ill and took to her bed suffering repeated bouts of diarrhoea and vomiting. Within two weeks she was dead and buried. Seddon, as her executor, opted for the briefest funeral and the cheapest interment (and possibly even accepted a percentage from the undertaker for introducing a new client).

On the understanding that he was now expected to look after two more children, Seddon wasted little time in taking over Barrow's remaining investments – the better, he claimed, to discharge his responsibilities as their new legal guardian. It was this final move on the part of the avaricious Seddon which was to prove his downfall.

It was to be his misfortune that Miss Barrow had some family, namely the Vonderahes, in nearby Evershot Road. They were keen to discover what had become of their dead cousin's estate – and quite possibly hoping to inherit it. They found Seddon unhelpful and obstructive. Sensing foul play, the Vonderahes requested an exhumation and post-mortem, the latter seeming mostly to confirm that it was a death by natural causes apart from some slight traces of arsenic.

These threw the spotlight back onto Seddon, although there was of course no evidence to show that Seddon or an accomplice had administered the poison. Subsequently, the court heard that one of the Seddon children had been sent out to buy some flypapers, and boiling a couple of these would be sufficient to procure a lethal dose. This was no more than circumstantial evidence, but their father had clearly profited from his association with the victim and he looked set to continue to do so following her death.

In response, Seddon argued, somewhat optimistically, that Eliza Barrow might accidentally have drunk the water in which the papers were dipped, while his barrister attempted to undermine the authority of the post-mortem findings. Unfortunately, when cross-examined by Sir Rufus Isaacs KC, Seddon's arrogant demeanour played badly with the jury and a guilty verdict was brought in.

At this point, the accused made one last extraordinary appeal for mercy – to the judge who he had identified as a brother Mason. Acknowledging his appeal and speaking with some emotion, Mr Justice Bicknell responded by telling Seddon:

> It is not for me to harrow your feelings – try to make peace with your Maker. We both belong to the same Brotherhood, and though that can have no influence with me this is painful beyond words to have to say what I am saying, but our Brotherhood does not encourage crime, it condemns it.

Seddon was duly hanged at Pentonville Prison on 18 April 1912.

HAWLEY HARVEY CRIPPEN

39 Hilldrop Crescent, N7 (1910)
30 Constantine Road, NW3 (1910)

The Classic English Murder

Poor old Dr Crippen killed only once, but more than a century on his crime is still one of the most notorious in London's long history, and his slightly strange and sinister name rarely fails to get top billing in books on the history of English murder. It helps that his tale is a classic love triangle, with some low-level glamour thrown in – his wife was an amateur music hall artiste – together with a bit of cross-dressing. Also, of course, the excitement of new technology, with a new shipborne telegraphy system being used to alert the authorities to Crippen and his lover's presence on the SS *Montrose*.

Add to this the thrilling cat-and-mouse aspect of the chase, with Scotland Yard officers racing across the Atlantic to greet the suspect as he disembarks, and the story has all the hallmarks of an enjoyable film. It helps, too, that the individuals involved are all characters we can recognise: the joyless, bossy and domineering wife; a henpecked husband who against all odds dares to take a lover; and the exotic sounding Ethel Le Neve who, to the husband's great delight, is happy to take him on.

Crippen had an American qualification in homeopathy which entitled him to call himself 'doctor' but not to practise when he arrived in Britain from Michigan in 1900. Instead, he took to selling patent cures from an address in New Oxford Street, being forced to do the housework when he returned home to Hilldrop Crescent each evening by his bullying, over-bearing wife.

Cora was Crippen's second wife. The first had been a tortured soul who was reportedly in the habit of racing off to confession immediately following those rare occasions when they shared a bed. Her replacement, who appeared on stage under the name Bella Elmore, had no such qualms but enjoyed the experience of having Crippen under her thumb and would taunt him whenever and wherever she could.

In 1910, Crippen reached breaking point and, having formed an attachment to his secretary Ethel, poisoned Cora with hyoscine on 1 February, dissected the body and concealed it in the coal cellar. He took the precaution of packing the flesh in lime to speed the process of decay and circulated the story that she had died while on a trip back home to the USA. This was que-ried, particularly given the speed with which Ethel had moved in to No. 39, but not to any great depth, as the disappearance in America of an American's American wife was not in itself particularly remarkable.

Crippen and Ethel took fright, however. When questioned by Inspector Walter Dew, Crippen had managed to persuade the detective that he had made up the story about Cora's death in order to cover his shame at being cuckolded and deserted. But they fled nevertheless, and it was this which really aroused suspicion.

Disguised as Mr and Master Robinson, they boarded the *Montrose*. The captain had his interest piqued by how unusually affectionate they seemed for two Edwardian-era males, and by Ethel's ill-fitting costume. The police, meanwhile, on another search of No. 39, finally uncovered some human remains wrapped in some pyjamas. Crippen had mistakenly added water to his lime, thereby preserving Cora's flesh rather than hastening its decomposition.

When Captain Kendall read of this, he put two and two together, sending a wireless message or 'marconigram' to Scotland Yard voicing his suspicions. Dew quickly moved to book a passage on a much faster vessel, the *Laurentic*, and so was able to apprehend both defendants when they stepped ashore at Quebec.

During Crippen's week at sea, his notoriety had grown like Topsy. Kendall used the joyous wonder of wireless to keep the press informed about the lovers' movements, complete with tempting titbits about their behaviour and their personal effects. This, of course, did much to set the tone for the case, with the two attempting to live a life of blameless domesticity behind the quiet, genteel façade of No. 39 – knowing all the while that the rotting corpse of the victim lay beneath their feet.

Now aged 47, and apparently even relieved at being caught, Crippen made no attempt to deny his part in the crime and was hanged at Pentonville on 23 November. Le Neve was subsequently acquitted as an accessory, and after marrying an accountant she lived on until 1967. Unfortunately, No. 39 and its neighbours were destroyed by enemy action in the 1940s (and later replaced by a block of flats named after Margaret Bondfield MP), but Le Neve's previous digs at No. 30 Constantine Road still survive.

GEORGE JOSEPH SMITH

14 Waterlow Road, N19 (1915)

'I Don't Want Any Walking, Get it Over as Quick as You Can'

Just before Christmas 1914, the *News of the World* carried the tragic story of newly married Margaret Lloyd (née Lofty) who had been found drowned in her bath in what had been called Bismarck Road in Highgate before the war with Germany led to its renaming. The report attracted the attention of Mr Charles Burnham, who was drawn to the story as his daughter Alice had died in a similar fashion a year before, shortly after she had married George Joseph Smith.

That marriage had also been brief, with Alice marrying Smith very much against her parents' wishes. Burnham indeed had never liked Smith at all, nor had he been persuaded by the manner of his daughter's death. This new report in the newspaper seemed to bear out his belief that there was definitely something more to what he saw as his erstwhile son-in-law's 'very evil appearance'.

Burnham's unease was shared by Joseph Crossley in Blackpool, Alice's landlord at the time of her death, who wrote to Detective Inspector Arthur Neil in London expressing his concerns about a number of parallels between the two deaths. On both occasions, the bereaved husband had quickly skipped town after the simplest possible funeral, even telling the undertaker at one of them, 'I don't want any walking, get it over as quick as you can.'

DI Neil also thought these similarities interesting, as well as finding it hard to credit that it would even be possible for an adult to drown accidentally in as small a bath as he found at Highgate. Investigations also revealed that the former Miss Lofty had emptied her Post Office account on the very day she had died and visited a local solicitor to make a will naming her new husband as the sole beneficiary.

Neil bided his time, however, until the Coroner's Office contacted him saying a communication had been received from a life insurance firm asking for details about Margaret's death. Her life had been insured for the handsome sum of £700.

After a short delay, Neil asked the coroner to file a report suggesting that the death was not suspicious. Arrangements were then made to keep watch on the solicitor's office, and on 1 February when 'Mr Lloyd' arrived to collect what was due to him the police moved in. Having ascertained that he was claiming to be both John Lloyd and George Joseph Smith, they arrested him, initially on a charge of bigamy.

Meanwhile, newspaper reports about these so-called 'Brides in the Bath' murders had suggested a link to yet another death dating back to July 1912. On that occasion, Bessie Williams was found drowned in her bath in Herne Bay, and once again her will had only recently been changed, leaving the enormous sum of £2,579 to her new husband. Calling himself Henry Williams on that occasion, Smith had been questioned about the death but had been allowed to walk free when a medical report suggested that Bessie had suffered a fit in the bath.

The resemblances between the three deaths were too strong to ignore. Indeed, much of the significance of these murders is that they represent one of the first occasions in the history of forensic pathology and detection that similarities between different crimes were used to build a case against the defendant. This was to be a technique used in numberless subsequent prosecutions, and it proved devastatingly effective in stopping George Joseph Smith.

In time, more information came to light about Smith, who had pursued a criminal career from his earliest days in Bethnal Green's Roman Road. By age 25, he had been imprisoned three times for theft. Married once legally, in 1898, he had since gone on to marry no fewer than eight different women bigamously, on each occasion fleeing after robbing them of what money they possessed and – where necessary – killing them to collect life insurance or whatever was left to him in their wills.

Finally brought to the Old Bailey on 22 June and charged with all three murders, Smith was told by the presiding judge Mr Justice Scrutton that he was so callous that 'an exhortation to repentance would be wasted on you'. The jury had taken just twenty minutes to find him guilty and the judge sentenced him to death. He was hanged at Maidstone Gaol on 13 August 1915.

JOE MEEK

304 Holloway Road, N7 (1967)

Pop's Own Space-Age Pioneer

Few murderers have their own, entirely respectable appreciation society. However, known as the 'alchemist of pop' and described time and again – wholly without irony – as Britain's Phil Spector, Robert George Meek's brief but successful and enormously influential career as a music producer was always going to mark him out from the crowd.

Meek's cramped, chaotic flat in this busy but shabby stretch of north London was where he lived, worked and died, sound-proofing the place as best he could with only limited means and making his name with The Tornados and 'Telstar'. Chosen by Lady Thatcher as one of her eight 'Desert Island Discs', in 1963 this had been the first single by a British group to chart at No. 1 in the USA.

A friend of Brian Epstein's and, like him, living very much on the wrong side of the law before the impact of the 1957 Wolfenden Report, Meek famously turned down the opportunity to work with The Beatles, instead preferring to plough his own furrow. He had previously worked as an engineer for the Midlands Electricity Board but now, self-taught and with financial backing from the improbably named Major Wilfred Alonzo Banks, he struck out to become one of this country's first independent record producers.

As a pioneer of space-age pop, Meek was an innovator but highly eccentric. Placing musicians wherever he could find space for them in the flat, and treating the studio itself as an instrument, he frequently dismantled electrical equipment to see what he could do with it and would play tapes backwards to create weird sounds that no one else had yet thought of.

Huge hits followed as a result of his uninhibited explorations, but Meek was clearly already a troubled individual. He was raised as a girl for his first four years by a mother in the Forest of Dean who had always wanted a daughter, and then dismissed as a sissy once he started school. His persecution complex was perhaps understandable but sat dangerously with a growing interest in the occult.

Meek, said friends after his death, would frequent graveyards, attempt to record the voices of the dead, and claimed to be in touch with the spirit of his hero, Buddy Holly. At other times, he insisted that Decca Records were bugging his flat in order to steal his ideas. (Those ideas subsequently led author and fan Jake Arnott to memorialise him as the man whose mad genius 'transformed cheap pop music into something wildly expressionistic and strangely ethereal'.)

By August 1966, he had money worries too, as his style of music was gradually pushed into the background by the blistering success of Dylan's *Blonde on Blonde* album, which was released on 12 August, and The Beatles' *Revolver*. Worse still, while one new Meek production was dismissed by reviewers as 'a whistleable little melody of promise ... good of its kind and doubtless a hit three years ago, but not for today's market', copyright difficulties over another threatened to push him into bankruptcy.

Things worsened over the winter, and then still more so on 16 January 1967 with the discovery of a mutilated male body dumped in two suitcases in a field near Tattingstone, Suffolk. Convinced that he would be implicated in the death – although there is no evidence that he had anything to do with it – Meek's behaviour became increasingly erratic when the victim was identified as a teenager who was said to have hung around the studio at No. 304.

With the pressure building, another of his records was written off by a critic as 'a corny bit of beat'. Meek displayed many of the symptoms of someone suffering from an amphetamine-induced psychosis and events came to a head a couple of weeks later. Dressed in black, he burst in on a group of friends, telling them he was possessed. The following morning, after fatally wounding his landlady Violet Shenton, Meek turned a shotgun on himself.

The date was 3 February 1967, the eighth anniversary of Buddy Holly's death in a plane crash and a coincidence which is lost on no one who follows the arc of Meek's career. Perhaps even more remarkable, however, is the final morbid parallel with the life of Phil Spector – another wayward recording genius with a gun, and one who, decades later, was convicted of the murder of Lana Clarkson. She was shot dead on 3 February 2003.

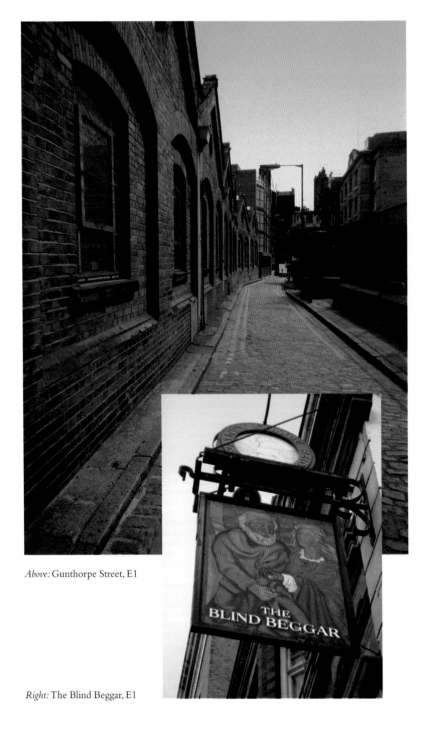

Above: Gunthorpe Street, E1

Right: The Blind Beggar, E1

Above: Cinnamon Street, E1

Left: Cutler Street, E1

Above: Carlton Gardens, SW1

CITY OF WESTMINSTER

WILLIAM TERRISS
1847 ~ 1897

HERO OF THE ADELPHI
MELODRAMAS

MET HIS UNTIMELY END
OUTSIDE THIS THEATRE
16 DEC 1897

THE ADELPHI THEATRE CO. LTD

Right: Maiden Lane, WC2

Above: Caxton Hall, SW1

Right: Lower Belgrave Street, SW1

Hammersmith Bridge

Blackfriars Bridge

Above: Savoy Hotel, WC2

Right: Charing Cross
Hotel, WC2

Cecil Court, WC2

Wellington Square, SW3

Left: Pembroke Gardens, W8

Right: The Goat, W8

Left: Lexham Gardens, W8

Below: Harrington Gardens, SW7

Onslow Square, SW7

Above: Hilldrop Crescent, N7

Right: Holloway Road, N7

JOE MEEK
RECORD PRODUCER
"THE TELSTAR MAN"
1929 — 1967
PIONEER OF SOUND
RECORDING TECHNOLOGY
LIVED, WORKED AND
DIED HERE

Noel Road, N1

Melrose Avenue, NW2

Agar Grove, NW1

Right: Downshire Hill, NW3

South Hill Park, NW3

Left: South Hill Park, NW3

Below: Morden College, SE3

Waterloo Road, SE1

St Oswalds Place, SE11

Lower Road, SE16

Left: Bedford Hill,
SW12

Below: Clapham
Common, SW4

Above: HMP Wandsworth, SW18

Above: Wormwood Scrubs, W12

Left: Bartle Street, W11

JOE ORTON

25 Noel Road, N1 (1967)

'If You Read this Diary All Will be Explained'

Joe Orton's death was discovered on 9 August 1967 after a chauffeur arrived at the top-floor flat in Noel Road to take the celebrated playwright to a script meeting at Twickenham Studios. He had been beaten with a hammer.

After ringing and failing to get an answer, the chauffeur peered through the letterbox. He was surprised to see the lights still on – it was nearly midday – and doubtless even more surprised to see the naked, bloodied body of a man lying on the hall floor.

The body belonged to 40-year-old Kenneth Halliwell, Orton's partner of more than fifteen years. The two had met at RADA in the 1950s, after which both had been keen to take on literary London, this despite – or more probably in the face of – an assessment of the schoolboy Orton as an eleven-plus failure who was merely 'semi-literate'. Halliwell's early years seem to have been slightly better spent – he had taken a Higher Schools Certificate – but for both, the early years had their ups and downs, including menial jobs, periods of poverty and a spell in prison for defacing many hundreds of library books.

Both had ambition, but success came first to Orton with his 1964 play, *Entertaining Mr Sloane*. This and *Loot*, two years later, badly upset the partnership of equals which had for years existed between the two of them. With an unproduced play to his credit and half a dozen unpublished novels, Halliwell's growing sense of failure coincided perfectly with Orton's new-found celebrity. In January 1967, Orton's diary described a meeting with Paul McCartney – he was also in talks about writing a screenplay for a new Beatles film – and it was rapidly becoming apparent that while the Establishment might be happy to accommodate Orton's homosexuality, Halliwell was not well suited to play the role of writer's wife.

Fast-forward a few months, and a quick look around the flat on that August morning uncovered another body in the bedroom of the flat. This was Orton himself, although horrific injuries to the face meant that the 34-year-old was eventually identified only by a tattoo of a bird over an old appendectomy scar. He had been battered to death with nine hammer blows from the blood-spattered Halliwell, who in turn – it transpired – had then swallowed nearly two dozen Nembutal tablets before collapsing in the hall. Autopsies confirmed that Halliwell had actually died first, after washing down the tablets with a can of grapefruit juice.

Halliwell's motive was confirmed by a suicide note, which advised the reader, 'If you read this diary all will be explained – K.H. PS. Especially the latter parts.' Clearly, as Orton's star had risen the balance of the two men's relationship had tipped irreversibly. Halliwell was intensely jealous of Orton's success and frustrated by his own lack of it. Orton may well have felt himself under pressure to break off the relationship, and it was certainly clear from his diary that he was enjoying flaunting his new fame and a more promiscuous lifestyle in a manner which badly upset Halliwell.

Already concerned that he was being eased out of Orton's life, Halliwell must have read with horror diary entries describing their rows – 'exhausting wrangles over trivia' – and observing how he, Orton, was shining in company whereas Halliwell was increasingly just aggressive, withdrawn and rude to his boyfriend's famous friends. The diaries also provided proof that Orton no longer found the physical side of their relationship at all fulfilling, and entry after entry reveals a casual approach to infidelity with Orton seeking satisfaction all over north London. One entry in particular described in detail a veritable orgy in a public lavatory on the Holloway Road – exactly the kind of encounter Halliwell could not stand.

In the decades since his death, it has often been observed that the macabre circumstances of Orton's death could well have found a place in one of his own dark comedies. Certainly reading his diary, Halliwell might well have drawn a horrifying connection between his own life and the way in which Orton was able to use depictions of such appetites as lust and greed to spotlight the bleak emptiness and essential loneliness of human life.

According to friends, the playwright would never have left Halliwell, despite their rows, the furious demands for Orton to control his taste for casual sex, and Halliwell's obvious jealousy and possessiveness. Perhaps it is fortunate that, in the end, Orton's threats to do so were never put to the test. After being cremated at Golders Green, the ashes of the two men were mingled and buried together. Today a plaque marks the house in this quiet, sunlit street.

DENNIS NILSEN

23 Cranley Gardens, N10 (1983)
195 Melrose Avenue, NW2 (1983)

'I was Desperate for Company, Even if it was Only a Body'

An army chef and trainee police constable before settling down to a superficially unremarkable life as a junior clerk in the Civil Service, Nilsen succeeded in killing and concealing more victims than would seem plausible in a city as large and as densely populated as late twentieth-century London. In fact, the opposite may be true: it could probably have happened nowhere else.

No less incredible was Nilsen's complicity in the actions which trapped him in the end, making such a clumsy effort to cover up after fellow tenants had called in a plumbing company to unblock the drains which turned out to be clogged with human remains. When arresting officers tentatively asked whether he had killed one or two people, Nilsen – visibly relieved at being arrested – astonished them by replying 'fifteen or sixteen'.

His story begins several years previously and a short drive away at 195 Melrose Avenue in Cricklewood. Nilsen, a lonely, heavy-drinking homosexual, moved there in the late 1970s with Bleep, a one-eyed mongrel. On 30 December 1978, he killed the first of his twelve victims, Stephen Holmes (whom he had met in the Cricklewood Arms), using a necktie to strangle him and then dunking his head into a bucket of water. Nilsen concealed the corpse under the floorboards, waiting eight months until the smell drove him to remove the body to the back garden, where it was incinerated on a bonfire.

With a little variation, this was a pattern he was to repeat eleven times over the next three years, interring each victim under the floor and only later burning their remains on local waste ground when the smell got too bad. On two occasions he was almost caught, when a couple of would-be victims escaped. One declined to press charges, and the police dismissed the other thinking the whole thing was no more than a lovers' tiff.

The truth is, intentionally or not, Nilsen tended to select his victims well, alighting on marginal, homosexual drifters from among a shifting, anonymous population – individuals unlikely to be reported missing by caring families or arouse suspicion by not turning up for work. Consequently, when Nilsen accepted £1,000 to move out in 1981, he seemed to have got away with it, and might indeed have done so had his murderous drive not travelled with him from Cricklewood to what was then a rather seedy and dilapidated part of Muswell Hill.

At Cranley Gardens, he and Bleep found themselves living in a top-floor flat, meaning no more corpses could be stored under the floor. Before long, Nilsen had devised a solution, still choosing to strangle his victims with a tie or drown them, but now dismembering the corpses and cooking up the remains before disposing of them piecemeal.

Some body parts were flushed down the lavatory, others rendered on the kitchen stove, and some simply left out in black binbags on the street for the dustmen to cart away. Three more victims disappeared this way – all relative strangers whom

Nilsen befriended in West End pubs – before his fellow tenants began to complain about the blocked drains.

The law finally caught up with him on 7 February 1983. Nilsen was arrested shortly after returning home from his work at an employment office in Kentish Town. Immediately admitting his guilt (and telling the police about two plastic bags in his wardrobe which contained more human remains), a defence of 'diminished responsibility' seemed most likely once detectives had retraced Nilsen's steps back to Cricklewood and started digging around in Melrose Avenue.

In layman's terms, Nilsen's actions were certainly those of a madman, and the hope must have been to bring in a verdict for manslaughter rather than murder. But in the event, the defence team failed to make this connection, and at the Old Bailey on 4 November 1983, less than three weeks before his 38th birthday, Dennis Andrew Nilsen was convicted of six murders and two attempted murders after twelve hours of deliberation. The judge recommended a minimum of twenty-five years, which was later raised to a whole-life tariff. Bleep was to spend his remaining days at Battersea Dogs' Home.

It took until 2005 before Stephen Holmes could be positively identified, and incredibly, nearly three decades after his conviction, seven of the fifteen victims are still unknown – a sad reflection on the short, chaotic and disconnected lives they all must have led. Nilsen claimed he was merely 'desperate for company, even if it was only a body', but his motives are even now not really clear at all.

7

NORTH-WEST LONDON

PHYLLIS DIMMOCK

29 Agar Grove, NW1 (1907)

'What Shall We Do to Pay the Rent?'

That the violent and bloody death of Phyllis Dimmock remains unsolved has caused comparisons to be drawn between the activities of Jack the Ripper in Whitechapel and the perpetrator of what came to be known as the Camden Town Murder – although the two are separated by several miles and a good two decades.

A Hertfordshire publican's daughter, born Emily Elizabeth Dimmock, 1907 saw the victim and her partner living together in rented digs in what was then St Paul's Road. She styled herself Mrs Bertram Shaw, although there is no evidence to suggest that the two were ever legally married.

Shaw himself was employed as a cook on one of the overnight services of the Midland Railway, Dimmock filling the long hours of his absence and earning a few shillings by working locally as a prostitute. Favourite pick-ups were The Rising Sun at No. 120 Euston Road and The Old Eagle in Royal College Street, although it was her habit to entertain clients a few minutes' walk away at home.

Both pubs are still there today, and Dimmock is known to have visited both prior to her husband's return from Derby on the morning of 12 September. He found her naked and mutilated corpse on the floor of their flat. Her throat was cut from

137

ear to ear, the flat had been ransacked, and the time of death was put at somewhere in the early hours.

Investigations soon revealed that on three of the preceding four evenings the deceased had been at The Rising Sun with another cook called Robert Roberts. She had excused herself on the fourth occasion by showing him a postcard suggesting that she had a prior engagement for the evening so could not meet him. Roberts, it quickly transpired, had a reliable alibi for the night of the 11th, so the postcard – discovered at No. 29 as the unhappy railwayman started to clear up – seemed to offer the best chance of catching the murderer.

Instead of naming the pub in question, the card included a little sketch showing a cheerful sun rising over the horizon and winking broadly at the reader. It was signed 'Alice', but when it was published in the *News of the World* the style and handwriting caught the eye of another prostitute, Ruby Young, who – possibly inadvertently – fingered a former boyfriend and graphic artist called Robert Wood.

Wood was soon charged with murder and hauled into court where, by very great fortune, he was to be defended by one of the great advocates of his age, the aforementioned Sir Edward Marshall Hall. Wood, however, was a shockingly bad witness. Striking a self-consciously superior pose, he refused to answer even the most straightforward questions from his own counsel, such as: 'Mr Wood, did you kill Emily Dimmock?' On being asked the same question a second time, Wood affected to find it ridiculous, leading some to suggest that his juvenile posturing might have been sufficient to persuade the jury that he was incapable of committing such a crime.

A more likely suggestion is that Sir Edward won the day for him, however, as his performance in the case won him the title among his peers of 'the Great Defender'. Either way, it took the jury just fifteen minutes to acquit Wood; a surprising outcome, especially as the judge, Mr Justice Grantham, had been expected to use his summing up to indicate his own desire to convict Wood.

With no other evidence to direct them, the police moved on and the public gradually lost interest. As a consequence, Dimmock might not even be remembered today, were it not for the spurious 'Ripper' connection and what looks like an early attempt to cash in on the publicity surrounding the case by the German-born impressionist Walter Sickert.

For some years, Sickert had been painting a series of ordinary domestic interiors, and had produced a number of works depicting sombre, reflective-looking nudes lying on beds. Following the trial, he exhibited a group of four such paintings under the collective title of the *Camden Town Murder*, including one showing a man staring down at the floor with the lifeless figure of a naked woman immediately behind him.

The resulting controversy certainly succeeded in raising his artistic profile, and today the group of four number amongst Sickert's best-known works. In one very real sense, however, the move can be said to have backfired, as recently a number of books have appeared suggesting Sickert himself was Phyllis Dimmock's killer and even, according to some, the Ripper himself.

That Sickert, like Roberts, could produce alibis seems no longer to matter, nor that the paintings had earlier appeared with entirely different titles. One was simply called *Summer Afternoon* and the one with the man in it, *What Shall We Do to Pay the Rent?*, which puts a very different spin on the image but has done little to rescue Sickert's posthumous reputation.

ALAN CHAPPELOW

The Manor, 9 Downshire Hill, NW3 (2006)

A Familiar, if Eccentric Figure Around Hampstead

Born in Copenhagen but raised in London, author and photographer Chappelow moved into Downshire Hill as a boy and – aside from a few years at boarding school in the Fens and Trinity College, Cambridge – he lived there until his 86-year-old body was found battered and bloodied under piles of personal papers in 2006.

One of the first western tourists to visit the USSR after the Second World War, Chappelow had worked briefly for the *Daily Mail* and *Daily Telegraph* in the 1950s as a photographer, taking portraits of leading figures in the arts. Latterly something of a recluse, today his reputation relies on two volumes of a biography of George Bernard Shaw with whom he formed a notable friendship.

Having lived in the manor for the best part of three-quarters of a century, Chappelow cut a familiar if eccentric figure around Hampstead, reportedly refusing to have a telephone in the house and making his rare forays to the local library astride a 1940s motorbike. According to neighbours, and regardless of the weather, Chappelow would make these excursions dressed in a leather helmet and an old mac tied closed with a length of string. 'Never very domestically inclined', he also made attempts to repair the Georgian property himself, using plastic bags in place of missing roof slates and securing loose guttering with sticky tape.

In June 2006, police called at the house after being alerted by Chappelow's bank, which had been unable to contact him following a series of suspicious transactions involving one of his accounts. With the front garden by now heavily overgrown and the path blocked by vegetation and an assortment of junk, the police gained entry to find the author under a 3ft pile of papers. Blood was spattered a metre and a half up the walls, and the torso was covered in wax and burns.

Evidence that Chappelow's post had been tampered with seemed to indicate that he was a victim of identity theft, but it subsequently proved impossible to date his killing with any accuracy. In October, however, police announced that a suspect had been arrested in Switzerland, and a 43-year-old financial trader called Wang Yam was subsequently extradited and charged with battering the author to death, stealing his identity and raiding his bank accounts.

As far as a motive was concerned, the accused was known to have money difficulties, and after being declared bankrupt as long ago as 2004 had been facing eviction from a property in a neighbouring street. In early 2007, the case took an unexpected turn, however, when the *Evening Standard* reported that Home Secretary Jacqui Smith was seeking to have part of the trial held in secret on the grounds of national security.

The defendant, the Old Bailey court was told, had been one of the leaders of the 1989 Tiananmen Square uprising and part of his defence was expected to involve his work for the intelligence service, MI6. On 14 January 2008 the necessary gagging order was granted, an unprecedented move in a case involving murder, burglary and deception, with the trial set to commence two weeks later.

On 31 March the case reached its conclusion. The defendant was convicted of obtaining a £20,000 money transfer by deception and stealing £20 from a cash machine by an eleven to one majority. The following day, the jury found the same individual also guilty of handling stolen goods in relation to a mobile phone, four blank cheques and cash. Thereafter, in the absence of any reliable forensic evidence and unable to reach verdicts in relation to charges of murder or burglary, they were discharged by the trial judge, Mr Justice Ouseley.

A retrial was ordered for 13 October, when the case for the prosecution would be held in public but the case for the defence would be in camera. In the event, the prosecution took eight weeks to tell its side of the story, producing CCTV evidence of a credit card in Chappelow's name being used at the Curry Paradise restaurant in South End Green.

Once again, the most serious charge was denied, but in his summing up Judge Ouseley told the jury that the Crown's case 'essentially found that the person who stole Mr Chappelow's identity was the same person responsible for the killing'. On 16 January 2009, the BBC reported that the former dissident – still insisting he was framed by 'men with no allegiance to this country', and with the police refusing to release a photograph of him for publication – had been convicted of Chappelow's murder and sentenced to twenty years.

More recently, permission has been granted for the listed but dilapidated Manor House to be dismantled and the site developed.

STANLEY SETTY

620b Finchley Road, NW11 (1949)

'I Hereby Confess to the *Sunday Pictorial* that I Stabbed Him to Death'

On 21 October 1949, a punt-gunner out after ducks near Tillingham in the Essex marshes chanced upon a waterlogged package. This turned out to contain a headless, legless human torso with five stab wounds visible on the chest.

An examination by the Home Office pathologist Professor Francis Camps indicated that the stab wounds accounted for the victim's death. Camps further stated that in his opinion the large number of broken bones suggested that the body may have been dropped from a substantial height.

Although the remains had been in the water for some time, the police were able to get prints from the victim's fingers and these matched a set they already had on file for a 44-year-old Baghdadi called Stanley Setty. A used-car dealer of decidedly questionable character, Setty's patch was in London, not Essex, and the police soon discovered he had gone missing more than two weeks previously along with £1,000 in £5 notes.

The serial numbers of the missing notes were circulated to the press and, acting on a hunch that the body might have been thrown from an aeroplane, the police started to ask around local flying clubs to see if anyone had seen anything suspicious. Very soon, a United Services Flying Club mechanic came up with something useful, recalling one of his members, Brian Donald Hume, manhandling a large package into an aeroplane before taking off from Elstree on 5 October.

Tracing Hume was easy enough, and he was promptly arrested at the flat that he shared with his wife and new baby above what was then a greengrocer's near Golders Green Station. The case against him was building nicely. The mechanic's story was backed up by evidence of damage to a window of the aircraft, the testimony of the taxi driver who had driven Hume back to London and been paid using some of Setty's money, and bloodstains in the flat which appeared to match the victim's blood type.

When he was interviewed at Albany Street Police Station, however, Hume vehemently denied any part in the man's murder, conceding only that he had been paid by three strangers to dump a large parcel into the sea. The three he could identify only as Mac, Greeny and The Boy, who he said had paid him £150 to do the job and keep mum.

Appearing at the Old Bailey on 18 January 1950, Hume stuck to this story that he was just the errand boy, and two days later the jury withdrew to consider the evidence, with the foreman returning after three hours to admit they could not reach a verdict. A second jury was sworn in, but they were formally ordered to find Hume not guilty of a charge of murder. It seemed the only charge he could be convicted on was being an accessory, in that he had admitted to disposing of the body.

Sentenced to twelve years, but released from Broadmoor after serving just eight, Hume promptly sold his story to the *Sunday Pictorial* for £3,600. For the time, it was a staggering sum. Hume cheerfully admitted to his nearly 6 million readers that, grasping an authentic SS dagger, a wartime souvenir, 'my sweating hand plunged the weapon frenziedly and repeatedly into his chest and legs'.

He was, he said, born with a chip on his shoulder as big as an elephant, and learned as a child that, 'if you have an enemy, get rid of him'. Unfortunately, this was something he proved again within weeks of his release, shooting a bank manager during a raid in Brentford and then – after fleeing to Switzerland – killing a taxi driver after an attempt on a bank in Zurich. The latter earned him sixteen years in a Swiss jail before he was sent back to Britain and returned to Broadmoor Hospital, where he was apparently a model patient.

In 1998 the *Sunday Mirror* reported that the 78-year-old, now released, had been found dead in the grounds of a Basingstoke hotel, apparently of natural causes.

RUTH ELLIS

The Magdala, South Hill Park, NW3 (1955)

'It is Obvious that When I Shot Him I Intended to Kill Him'

If it were not for the fact that Britain no longer exercises the right to hang convicted killers, the likelihood is that few of us would remember Ruth Ellis, the Welsh-born daughter of a Belgian émigré and a roving cruise-line cellist. The premeditated shooting dead of her lover, David Blakely, outside a Hampstead pub on Easter Sunday 1955 was certainly violent, and thirty years later it was to form the basis of an enjoyable film, *Dance With a Stranger*, starring Miranda Richardson. However, in most other regards it was a fairly commonplace story, a run-of-the-mill 'domestic', in police parlance, although the press at the time dressed things up a bit after detecting a whiff of a more engaging *crime passionnel*.

Ellis was a nightclub manageress and Blakely a racing driver, albeit not a very good one. The two had been introduced to each other by Britain's first ever Formula One World Champion, the sport's golden boy, Mike Hawthorn. This was precisely the sort of detail that lent the proceedings a much-needed touch of glamour.

The real interest in the case, however, was provided by the sentence passed down by the judge, Sir Cecil Havers – grandfather to *Chariots of Fire* and *Coronation Street* actor Nigel Havers – and the fact that Ellis was the last woman to be executed under English law.

Prior to this, the match between Ellis and Blakely had never been anything but tempestuous. Three days before the shooting they had been making love at her flat at No. 44 Egerton Gardens, Kensington, but the former nude model and divorced mother of two had taken another lover besides Blakely. Blakely was also apparently playing the field, clearly besotted by Ellis but almost certainly considering her to be beneath him socially.

When he failed to show up for a date on Good Friday, Ellis tracked him down to Hampstead, where she watched him leaving a party with a girl on his arm. Two days later, having fortified herself with a bottle of Pernod and an old .38 service revolver, she waited outside the Magdala and when Blakely stepped outside shot him dead. 'FOUR BULLETS AS HE LAY DYING' was the headline in the *Daily Mail*, although the additional bullet holes that for years could be seen in the tiled façade of this friendly Victorian pub were almost certainly faked by a canny landlord.

On the basis of these brief details, a sentence of death seemed assured, and one was duly handed down at the Old Bailey in June of that year. In fact, the all-women's prison at Holloway had already seen a number of such executions – including one barely six months earlier (see Styllou Christofi below) – and Ellis looked set to become the fifteenth woman hanged in England during the course of the twentieth century.

Despite this not inconsiderable total, the idea of hanging a woman has always been considered somehow more shocking than executing a man. In part because of this, a 50,000-signature petition was handed in to the Home Office.

At the appointed hour of 9 a.m. on 13 July, a large crowd assembled outside the prison, suggesting that this was a rather more controversial case than most. The jury had taken just twenty-three minutes to find Ellis guilty, and many observers concluded that in the USA, France, and even across the border in Scotland, the accused would have drawn a custodial sentence instead. Among the many who felt compelled to protest publicly was the novelist Raymond Chandler, who launched a blistering attack on the authorities in a letter to the London *Evening Standard*, describing what he called the 'medieval savagery of the law'.

Ellis herself had refused to appeal against the sentence, however. In fact, had she done so, her declaration to the prosecuting counsel Christmas Humphreys QC that, 'it is obvious that when I shot him I intended to kill him', might well have undermined any plea that she was only guilty of manslaughter. Her choice of weapon was also somewhat problematic: in court, she insisted she had owned it for years but never used it, although a forensic examination indicated very clearly that it had been cleaned and oiled immediately before the attack. (Indeed, later, while awaiting execution, Ellis reportedly changed her story. In the condemned cell, she admitted to her solicitor that the Smith & Wesson had been obtained for this express purpose, although the confession came too late and the authorities took no further action.)

Following her execution, and in line with normal practice at the time, the 29-year-old's body was buried in an unmarked grave within the prison grounds. Later, in 1971 during rebuilding work at HMP Holloway, permission was sought and obtained to remove her remains to St Mary's Church in Amersham – barely half a dozen miles from the Blakely family home at Penn and the final resting place of her erstwhile lover and victim.

Today, the chief legacy of the Ellis case is that it added considerable fuel to the fire for those organisations already seeking the abolition of the death penalty in Britain. Interestingly, one of those who in time came to support this movement was the aforementioned Christmas Humphreys QC, an early convert to Zen Buddhism (his former home at No. 58 Marlborough Place in St John's Wood is now a monastery). He famously prosecuted not just Ellis but also Timothy Evans, Derek Bentley and Christopher Craig, and the Cold War 'atom spy', Klaus Fuchs.

STYLLOU CHRISTOFI

11 South Hill Park, NW3 (1954)

'Please Come. Fire Burning. Children Sleeping.'

By quite remarkable coincidence, South Hill Park had been the scene of another fatal domestic the previous year, in which the leading player – a fiery-tempered, middle-aged Greek Cypriot – was to become the penultimate woman to hang for murder in this country.

Styllou Pantopiou Christofi had arrived in London in 1953, moving into the ground-floor flat at No. 11 with her son Stavros, a waiter, and his German wife of twelve years. By contemporary accounts, their marriage had been a happy one, but the arrival of the mother-in-law from hell soon put things under an intolerable strain.

Unable to speak English at all well (and apparently unwilling to learn), the 53-year-old Mrs Christofi disliked cold, grey London, strongly disapproved of the way her daughter-in-law Hella was raising her grandchildren, and lost no opportunity to pick a fight or disrupt the family's life in any way she could. Later it was discovered that she had considerable previous form here, having in her mid-twenties been charged with murdering her own mother-in-law after forcing open the woman's mouth and ramming home a flaming torch of some description. The resulting injuries must have been truly horrifying, but a Cypriot court found Christofi had no case to answer, perhaps concluding – who knows? – that the actions of a passionate and possessive young woman were only to be expected from a spirited individual with such a lively, Mediterranean temperament.

Unfortunately for Stavros and Hella, the passing years had not caused her to mellow one whit, and by 1954 – recognising that the two of them could no longer continue to share the same address – Hella said she was taking the children on a trip to Germany and Stavros should do whatever was necessary to pack his mother off back to Cyprus.

In fact, Hella's mother-in-law had also concluded that their situation could not be allowed to continue. However, she proposed an altogether more drastic solution, which she set in train on 29 July. She did this by first hitting the 36-year-old Hella over the head, and then strangling her while she lay unconscious on the kitchen floor.

A curious choice of weapon, the cast-iron ash plate from the kitchen range, was perhaps the first indication that Christofi's plan had not been especially well thought out. The second was her decision to incinerate the body in order to get rid of the evidence – an absurdly optimistic scheme, even allowing for the primitive state of forensic science in the mid-1950s, and highly impractical in such a heavily built-up residential area.

Undeterred by common sense, Christofi dragged Hella's body out of the back of the building and doused it with paraffin. Under the watchful eye of a neighbour, who was sitting reading at a window overlooking the Christofis' garden, she dropped a match on the body and then went back into the house to tidy up. As it happens, the neighbour assumed she was simply disposing of an old shop mannequin or tailor's dummy, and so felt no need to raise the alarm. However, Christofi felt otherwise, and after a few minutes, with the funeral pyre well underway in the garden, she rushed out into the street to buttonhole a stranger who she persuaded into the flat. 'Please come,' she told him in her halting English. 'Fire burning. Children sleeping.'

It seemed that her luck had run out, however. The passer-by quickly took stock of the bizarre circumstances in which he found himself, spying the remains of a body, and decided to call the police.

Finding herself in custody, Christofi immediately attempted to portray the whole thing as a ghastly accident, but again one is forced to question her optimism. Besides the forensic evidence, and the testimony of Stavros who refused ever again to visit or speak to his mother, her fate must have been sealed even without rumours reaching London from Cyprus about her earlier arrest.

Even so, it is tempting to suppose that certain details of the case –the choice of weapon, most obviously – might have enabled Christofi to mount some kind of a defence, perhaps on the grounds that it was an impetuous act of one woman striking out at another in the heat of an argument. The public had little time for such theories, however, and it is interesting to note that – compared to Ruth Ellis, whose actions were clearly premeditated – there was relatively little outcry when Christofi went to the gallows on 13 December 1954.

That she was a foreigner almost certainly played a role here, and of course locally Christofi's reputation would have been as something of a homewrecker or modern-day harpy. Certainly, her executioner Albert Pierrepoint was struck by the differing reactions to the two South Hill Park crimes, noting in his memoir that it was the 'blonde night-club hostess' who won the hearts of the public – one of whom even promised him £90 if he would refuse to hang Ruth Ellis – rather than the 'grey-haired and bewildered grandmother who spoke no English'.

8

SOUTH-EAST LONDON

EDMUND POOK

The Mitre, Greenwich High Road, SE10 (1871)
Morden College, St German's Place, SE3 (1871)
Kidbrooke Lane, SE9 (1871)

'My Poor Head, My Poor Head'

With immoral relations between a young master and servant, an unplanned pregnancy, peremptory dismissal once this had been discovered, and in the end a brutal killing with a hammer, the story that emerged after the discovery of a 17-year-old girl, battered and bleeding to death on Eltham Common, was a gift to the sensationalist press of the 1870s.

The eventual acquittal of the only suspect in the case aroused particularly strong feelings – strong enough for a crowd of several thousand to follow a cart through the streets of Greenwich, on which was mounted a grisly tableau showing the lifelike figure of 20-year-old Edmund Pook hoisting a hammer over the head of the servant girl, Jane Clousen. When the cart stopped outside the Mitre, a tavern opposite what was then No. 3 London Road, the crowd turned ugly, shouting and screaming abuse at the defendant's front door on the opposite side of the street.

Pook was employed in his father's printing business and at the time of the murder was still living under his parents' roof. On 13 April 1891, after two years' good service, Jane had been curtly dismissed by Mrs Pook. The reason given was her slovenly habits and appearance, but Mrs Pook had sensed something developing between her and Edmund and wanted to stop it.

Jane took lodgings a few hundred yards away in Ashburnham Place and, already pregnant, confessed to her landlady that the two were actually engaged. There is some suggestion that the pair arranged to meet in secret a couple of weeks after Jane's dismissal, but then on 27 April a policeman patrolling along Kidbrooke Lane (by the moated Tudor Barn, in what is now the gardens of Well Hall Pleasaunce) came upon a girl attempting to crawl along the road. She was, he said, quietly moaning, 'Oh, my poor head, my poor head.' On being taken to Guy's Hospital, she died shortly afterwards.

The wounds to her head were truly awful. A doctor's report produced at Edmund Pook's trial described their 'incised character', with cuts right down to the bone, fragments of bone 'lying quite loose' and the skull itself so badly damaged that 'the brain was discovered to be lacerated'. Further examination confirmed that she was indeed two months pregnant, although the baby was thought to have died *in utero*, some while before the attack.

The murder weapon was found quite a distance away in the gardens of the seventeenth-century Morden College, the distinctive plasterer's hammer having been wiped clean, although it still bore traces of blood. A shopkeeper at No. 186 Deptford High Street confirmed that he had sold the implement to a man matching Edmund Pook's description, and another witness claimed that he had seen a figure which might have been Pook hurrying along Kidbrooke Lane the previous evening.

When interviewed by police, Pook confirmed that he had indeed seen Jane the previous evening but she had been in the company of another man who he could not identify. It also emerged that the shopkeeper was mistaken about the buyer of the hammer. However, when bloodstains were found on Pook's clothing he was charged with Jane's murder, and after a hearing at the Coroner's Court the trial date was set for 10 July at the Old Bailey.

Newspaper coverage of the trial was extensive, the popular press tapping into a vein of resentment while risking a charge of libel (and even perverting the course of justice) by depicting a scenario which most readers would have recognised. Having got a servant into trouble and not wishing to marry beneath his dignity, the young gentleman had clearly bumped her off rather than facing up to his responsibilities.

The jury thought otherwise, however, and Pook was quickly acquitted when no evidence emerged of an improper relationship between himself and the girl. With the prosecution failing to produce any correspondence to show the two had remained in touch after Jane's dismissal, the verdict was greeted by cheers in the courtroom. Unfortunately, it was met by booing outside it, the sound of a large and unruly crowd now burning with anger at what they saw as a guilty middle-class man getting away with the murder of a poor servant girl.

As the mob would have heard none of the evidence, it seems fair to say that much of the fury and bitterness was based on hearsay rather than the facts, and the case is often cited as one of the earliest examples of trial by media. Pook attempted to return to his normal life but, keen to whip up sales, pamphleteers continued to harass the family in the months that followed, and after a couple of successful libel suits the Pooks eventually changed their names and fled the capital. Even then, London was to have the last word, and in the 1871 census the recording officer wrote one word next to the name of Jane Maria Clousen: 'MURDERED'.

THOMAS NEILL CREAM

Duke of Wellington, 81–83 Waterloo Road, SE1
(1891)

The Lambeth Poisoner

One of several names to be put in the frame for the Ripper killings (see p. 19), Thomas Neill Cream is distinguished from most in that he was at least a convicted murderer who hanged for his crimes. He is also occasionally reported to have confessed, uttering the words, 'I am Jack the Ri ...' as the trapdoor on the gallows fell away – although none of the official witnesses who were present at his execution claim to have heard any such thing.

He was, nevertheless, a thoroughly bad egg: a Scots-born doctor who trained at St Thomas' Hospital and then in Canada, returning across the Atlantic in 1891 to murder several prostitutes in London using strychnine.

In Canada he had relished his work as an abortionist, attracting the attention of the authorities when a patient was found dead on his premises with clear symptoms of chloroform poisoning, and then two years later when a patient died on the operating table. He soon skipped town to Chicago, where he started selling various quack remedies for epilepsy, but then killed his lover's husband after spicing up the brew with some additives of his own. When one of these turned out to be strychnine, and his lover turned state's evidence, he managed to escape the noose again but was sent to the Joliet Correctional Centre.

On his release, and now back in Britain, Cream stayed at a hotel in Fleet Street and frequented the prostitutes around Lambeth and Waterloo. Perhaps to cut down on travelling, he moved to new lodgings at No. 103 Lambeth Palace Road, and was next seen in the company of Ellen Donworth.

On 16 October, she was taken ill outside the Duke of Wellington on Waterloo Road, and her symptoms of nausea and convulsions ahead of her death led police to a diagnosis of strychnine poisoning. This was confirmed when a letter was received – penned by Cream, although this was not yet known – suggesting that her murderer was Lieutenant Frederick Smith MP, later the 2nd Viscount Hambledon and the heir to the W.H. Smith & Son fortune.

For the time being, Cream was in the clear, and on 20 October he struck again, picking up 27-year-old Matilda Clover in a pub called the Canterbury Arms and going back to her digs at No. 27 Lambeth Road. She, too, was dead the following morning, and once again the symptoms indicated strychnine poisoning, although for a while her death was not considered suspicious as she was notorious in the area as something of a drunk.

In fact, it was not until the arrival of another letter that the police really took notice. This time, the letter went to the Savoy Hotel, addressed to Lady Russell. It suggested that her estranged husband, the earl, was responsible for this latest killing. A second letter went to the eminent neurologist William Broadbent, before being hastily forwarded on to Scotland Yard as it contained a threat of blackmail.

There was still nothing to link the killings to Cream, however, and after a brief return trip across the Atlantic he was back in action again, offering a restorative capsule to another prostitute he had picked up in Leicester Square. However, becoming suspicious of his motives, Lou Harvey dropped the medication into the Thames. Two more working girls were less fortunate, and Emma Shrivell and Alice Marsh died shortly after Cream had visited them at their flat in Stamford Street.

Once again, the police received a letter, this time accusing another doctor of the crimes – Walter Harper, who had lodged with Cream while completing his studies. This finally established a link with Cream, who had also come under surveillance when his unusually detailed knowledge of the killings had aroused the suspicion of the police. While it was expressed as merely a professional interest in the medical aspects of the murder, Cream managed to sound like he was bragging, and once his distinctive, cross-eyed appearance was mentioned by a number of other prostitutes, it looked like the game was up.

Thereafter, it did not take long to build a case, particularly when his activities in North America came to light. After being charged and found guilty of the murder of Matilda Clover, Cream was sentenced to hang on 15 November 1892.

To the very great disappointment of Londoners, the execution was held inside Newgate rather than in full view out in the street, and an angry crowd of 5,000 is said to have gathered outside to protest at their being denied such a spectacle. Since then, the legend of his last-minute Ripper confession has continued to echo down the years, but the fact that he was in Joliet for the whole of 1888 is well documented and one can say with certainty that Thomas Neill Cream is definitely not our Jack.

GEORGE CHAPMAN

The Crown, 213 Borough High Street, SE1 (1902)

'I See You Got Jack the Ripper at Last'

George Chapman, whose real name was Seweryn Antonowicz Kłosowski, murdered three women, and is another who is frequently cited as a possible candidate for the Ripper killings. He enjoyed a substantially longer run at it, however – nearly five years, as opposed to Jack's few months – and as his posthumous reputation as 'the Borough Poisoner' suggests, he preferred an altogether different modus operandi to that of his more celebrated East End rival.

This last point is significant, not least because there is a considerable body of research showing that the majority of serial killers tend to find something which works for them and then stick with it. The Ripper liked to strangle and mutilate prostitutes, whereas Chapman preferred poisoning barmaids with antimony, and most authorities consider it highly unlikely that Kłosowski would suddenly have switched to this means having enjoyed ritually disembowelling his victims on the other side of the river.

Seweryn or Severin Kłosowski had first arrived in England sometime in the 1880s, a young married Catholic previously apprenticed to a surgeon in Poland but still unqualified and now working as a barber. He briefly relocated again, to the

USA, and on returning to London in 1892 was cohabiting with a woman named Annie Chapman, whose name he decided to adopt.

By 1895, he was married to Mary Spink (both of them bigamously) and running a public house together near Old Street which was called the Prince of Wales. Mary died on Christmas Day that year. At the time it was assumed to be of natural causes.

Three years later, Chapman remarried to a Bessie Taylor. Once again, this was a bigamous arrangement, on his part if not hers, and the two of them shortly afterwards left London to run a pub in Hertfordshire. In 1900, the pair returned to the city to take over the Monument Tavern in Union Street, Lambeth, but neither the premises nor the wife survived the move for long. Mrs Chapman died barely a year later, on St Valentine's Day, and shortly afterwards the Monument caught fire suspiciously close to the date on which Chapman's lease was due to expire.

Widowed again, Chapman moved one last time, taking over the Crown public house at No. 213 Borough High Street. A few weeks later, he announced his engagement to one of the barmaids there – Maud Marsh.

Ahead of this news, Maud's parents already had reason to be concerned about Chapman, who had lied to them about there being another family living above the bar, presumably in a bid to persuade them that their daughter would be quite safe living on the premises. Having agreed to this arrangement, they had received a letter from their daughter suggesting that she would be fired if she did not let her employer have his wicked way with her. This was followed by another letter saying that since writing the first one she had married Chapman in secret. By October 1902 she too was dead.

At this point, the suspicions of a local doctor and the alarm of the Marsh family prompted the police to make a closer examination of George Chapman's habit of losing wives. When they were exhumed, the previous two were found to have decomposed hardly at all, a peculiarity which was already recognised as one of the side effects of antimony poisoning.

Soon finding himself in the dock for murder, Chapman's defence collapsed when he was shown to have purchased quantities of an emetic medicine from a chemist. This was an antimony-rich potassium tartrate compound, known to cause severe paralysis and death if administered in high doses. Duly charged with the third murder, Chapman was convicted on 20 March 1903 and hanged at Wandsworth Prison after nineteen days. Unfortunately, his motives were never revealed.

Aside from choosing a different means to inflict death on his victims, George Chapman clearly killed women he knew well, while the Ripper almost certainly preyed on strangers. The link between the two has nevertheless proved enduring, depending for the most part on a chance remark from a retired police inspector, who congratulated one of Chapman's arresting officers, saying, 'I see you got the Jack the Ripper at last.'

The evidence for this is extremely slight, however. Chapman's Polish origins may have led to him being confused with one or other of two popular Ripper suspects, Aaron Kosminski and Nathan Kaminsky. Or possibly the comment was made in jest, after which it fed the fears of a public who were unable or unwilling to accept that the Ripper was still at large (and understandably chilled by the notion that anyone

– after such a bloodthirsty spree – was able simply to stop killing when he or she had had enough). However, no serious researchers have given the theory any credence at all, and if Jack's true identity is ever discovered it is highly unlikely to be the Borough Poisoner.

Now converted to educational use, the Crown is the only building associated with Chapman to have survived.

HARRY DOBKIN

St Oswalds Place, Kennington Lane, SE11 (1942)

Nagged All the Way to the Gallows

The myth of the Blitz is a strong one, with the notion burned into the national psyche that in Britain's hour of direst need, this country's finest hour, we stood alone against the Luftwaffe and the Nazi invaders and Londoners all dug deep and pulled together. In the shadow of the great dome of St Paul's – wreathed in smoke and rich in symbolism – we snatched victory from the jaws of defeat through a combination of patriotic pride, stoicism, teamwork and selfless endeavour.

The reality, inevitably, is more complicated and markedly less attractive: spivs thrived as the black market in rationed goods went unchecked; the royal family were loudly booed as they toured bomb-damaged streets; houses were looted wholesale; and pedestrians were frequently attacked and robbed under cover of the blackout. With the police so often called away to other duties, crimes generally soared, and in retrospect it seems obvious that even murders would have gone undetected when air raids offered so many new ways to conceal a killing and then the body.

For example, on 17 July 1942, when a workman helping to demolish the Vauxhall Baptist Chapel just off Kennington Lane lifted a slab and found a body, it was only natural to assume that it was simply another tragic victim of the air raid that had taken place the previous October and claimed in excess of 100 lives. Fortunately, even in wartime there were procedures to be followed, however, and after the body was examined at the Southwark Mortuary by the Home Office pathologist Keith Simpson, the police were reasonably confident they were looking at a murder.

Apart from anything else, the head had been separated from the body, the lower jaw was missing completely, all four limbs had been severed at the elbow or knee, and a blood clot in the throat suggested that the victim had been strangled rather than flattened by falling masonry or a blast. There was also evidence of a fire, suggesting an effort had been made to further obscure the victim's identity. The pattern of putrefaction seemed out of the ordinary too, and a search of the burial site revealed the presence of slaked lime, a mixture presumably employed to reduce the odour of a rotting body, but which – unlike quicklime – would have inhibited the natural decaying of a corpse.

Back in his laboratory at Guy's Hospital, Simpson was soon able to assert that the body belonged to a woman of between 40 and 50 years of age, just over 5ft tall and grey haired. She had, he said, been lying in the crypt of the chapel for between twelve and fifteen months.

Armed with this information, the police soon came up with a possible name for the victim. She was Rachel Dobkin, the estranged wife of an employee in a neighbouring law firm. She had gone missing approximately fifteen months previously, matched Simpson's rough description fairly closely, and was subsequently identified using dental records relating to her upper jaw.

Harry Dobkin was arrested shortly afterwards, and a tale emerged of an arranged marriage dating back to 1920. The couple had proved themselves to be incompatible almost immediately, and police heard about years of resentment revolving around the payment of child maintenance for a boy who had been conceived during the three short days that Rachel and Harry shared as man and wife.

The boy, of course, was now 20 years old, and Dobkin – never particularly regular with his payments – was no longer obliged, nor at all keen, to go on paying. On several occasions Rachel had attempted to squeeze more money out of him, and four times tried unsuccessfully to sue him for assault. By early April 1941, Dobkin presumably had had enough, and after the two of them were observed together on Good Friday at a café in Shoreditch, Rachel was never seen alive again.

Three days later, on the night of 14 April, there had been a small fire in the Baptist Chapel at Vauxhall, which was rather odd as there had been no air raid that night. Odder still was that Dobkin had failed to report it, since he was the firewatcher on duty that night and would ordinarily have been required to do so.

With the war on, however, this was overlooked, and but for the workman's grisly discovery fifteen months later Dobkin might have got away with it. Instead, he found himself in the dock at the Old Bailey, his barrister striving in vain to convince the jury that the body had been misidentified. Alas for Dobkin, the jury was having none of it and found him guilty on 17 November 1942. Dobkin was hanged at Wandsworth on 7 January the following year.

The site of the chapel, which stood opposite a charming little courtyard behind St Peter's, Kennington Lane, is now covered by several low-rise blocks of flats.

MUTESA II OF BUGANDA

Orchard House, Lower Road, SE16 (1969)

'I Doubt if He Could Have Afforded Four Bottles of Vodka. The Whole Thing Stank.'

It seems reasonable to suppose that few, if any, citizens of modern-day Uganda are familiar with Lower Road, Rotherhithe. But then, the likelihood is that they know no more or less about this otherwise undistinguished corner of south-east London than the residents of SE16 know about Buganda, the largest of the traditional kingdoms of the aforementioned East African republic.

Perhaps they should, however, for it was here, at dreary Orchard House, that the kingdom's erstwhile ruler – and the sometime President of Uganda – met his end.

The records show that Major General Sir Edward Frederick William David Walugembe Mutebi Luwangula Mutesa II – 'King Freddie' to his friends and to the gossip columnists of Fleet Street throughout much of the 1960s – died of alcohol poisoning, apparently after consuming at least four bottles of vodka in as many hours. Officially, the death was taken to be self-inflicted, although four decades on, the suspicion still lingers that having been exiled to Great Britain, the former *kabaka* or ruler of the ethnic Ganda people was summarily bumped off on the orders of powerful forces back home.

Educated at Magdalen College, Cambridge and later commissioned into the army as an officer of the Grenadier Guards, Freddie succeeded to the throne of Buganda on the death of his father in 1939. Over the course of the next thirty years, he is thought to have married eleven times and sired up to eighteen children.

At the time of his accession, Uganda was a British protectorate, and unfortunately by the late 1940s Freddie had managed to find himself on the wrong side of both his own people and their colonial overlords. His followers resented what they saw as his dangerous proximity to the British authorities, and HM Government took it badly when he opposed the 1951 proposal to merge the countries of British East Africa – Uganda, Kenya and Tanganyika – into a new federation.

In particular, the Ugandans wished to avoid coming under the control of Kenya's white settlers – something similar had already happened in Rhodesia – and things came to a head in 1953 when their *kabaka* was formally deposed by the British Governor Sir Andrew Cohen and sent into exile. In fact – as revealed by the *Sunday Telegraph* more than forty years later – the operation to remove him looked more like a judicial kidnapping. Downing Street despatched an RAF Handley-Page Hastings transport aircraft to Entebbe with instructions for the crew to bundle Freddie on board and get him out of the country as quietly as possible.

The Africans were naturally outraged at Whitehall's high-handed behaviour, and within two years the authorities here had given in to popular demand and flown Freddie – by now a popular hero – back home to be reinstated on his throne.

His good fortune was not to last long, however. When Uganda was granted independence in 1962, Freddie quickly fell afoul of the new ruler, Milton Obote, who initially allowed him to retain a measure of personal prestige but no real power. Declaring himself president in 1966 and sending Freddie back into exile, Obote went on to abolish Uganda's sub-kingdoms completely and with them any aspirations to which their ruling families might still have clung.

Freddie moved into the Savoy, where he became something of a minor celebrity, and later to a house in Eaton Place, until what was left of a government allowance was exhausted. Broke, broken down and banned from returning home to Africa, King Freddie then removed himself to this anonymous corner of Southwark.

By April 1968 – almost exactly two years after he had entertained the Queen Mother, Princess Margaret and Lord Snowdon at his own palace in Kampala – he was reported to be living on the dole, telling the press, 'I'm glad to say the odd friend slips me a fiver now and then.'

On 21 November 1969, poor King Freddie was found dead in the top-floor flat at Orchard House with four empty vodka bottles by his side. Friends refused to believe he had died by his own hand, however. Among them was an influential acquaintance from his Cambridge days. The BBC's foreign correspondent John Simpson had visited Freddie the previous day, finding him 'entirely sober and perfectly calm'. As he later recalled, 'I saw no sign of booze in the flat, and I doubt if he could have afforded four bottles of vodka. The whole thing stank.' The finger was pointed at Obote, but investigations went no further.

GEORGE FRANCIS

304 Lynton Road, London, SE1 (2003)

'There Was an Inevitability that He Would Come to a Sorry End'

South-east London can claim the dubious honour of London's first ever recorded murder: that of Aelfheah, or St Alphege, in 1012. As Archbishop of Canterbury, he was put to death by the Danes, and exactly 1,000 years later his name lives on in the dedication of the finest church in Greenwich.

George Francis lacks any such memorial, but as an associate of the Kray twins he is perhaps equally unlikely to be forgotten. Having survived the murder and mayhem those two inflicted on East London in the 1950s and 1960s, and being linked one way and another to a total of twenty gangland killings, in 2003 he was himself gunned down outside the yard of his haulage firm, Signed, Sealed & Delivered.

In fact his fame, such as it is, springs from more than one source, as Francis was also implicated in another widely reported and decidedly notorious crime. This was the 1983 Brink's-Mat bullion job; an undertaking frequently ranked alongside the Great Train Robbery, and liable to be described (if only by the easily impressed) as the sort of brilliant criminal enterprise that somehow makes heroes of those who would otherwise be dismissed as examples of your usual, everyday London villain.

Francis' violent death on 14 May was perhaps only to be expected; indeed, two days later the *Independent* newspaper described how 'as an old-time crook and associate of such criminal luminaries as the Krays, Kenneth Noye and the Great Train Robbers, perhaps there was an inevitability that George Francis would come to a sorry end'.

Definitely more of a *Sun* reader himself, on the morning in question Francis had just collected his daily paper when he was gunned down at around 5 a.m. as he leaned into his green Rover to get something out. He was shot four times, in the face, back, arm and hand, and his death bore all the signs of a professional gangland 'hit'. The gunmen had clearly been lying in wait for their target and several witnesses reported hearing tyres squealing as the two made their getaway.

This was the second time such an attempt had been made – in 1985, Francis had survived being shot in the chest at a pub he owned in Kent – and once again, as a police spokesman drily observed after he had been pronounced dead, there was 'no shortage of suspects'.

Of course, you can tell a lot about a man from the company he keeps and by the time he was 16, Francis, who was to collect a total of five convictions for violence, already had a reputation as a useful hard man. He was often seen around town with the likes of Ronnie and Reggie and the Richardsons, and guests at his daughter's wedding were to include at least two of the Great Train Robbers, Buster Edwards and Charlie Wilson.

In 1981, he was cleared of involvement in a huge cannabis-smuggling racket, and two years later watched as the swimming pool at his place in Kent was drained and dug up by police looking for the missing 6,800 gold bars from the Brink's-Mat robbery.

None were found, but in 1986 Francis spent a year in jail after being found in possession of forged banknotes. Shortly after his release he was in trouble again, this time collecting a sixteen-year sentence and a £300,000 fine for smuggling cannabis.

After he was released, he claimed to have gone straight, although he maintained close friendships with a number of notorious south London 'faces'. These included another member of the Brink's-Mat gang, Brian Perry, who was himself gunned down in 2002 outside a minicab firm in which he had an interest.

Perry's murder, evidently another professional hit, remains unsolved. However, in 2007 two ageing hitmen, John O'Flynn and Terence Conaghan, were found guilty of killing Francis and jailed for a minimum of twenty years.

The two, who between them had more than 120 previous convictions, were caught after O'Flynn got drunk and started bragging to a girlfriend. Thereafter, an abundance of forensic evidence – including a discarded cigarette end and lots of CCTV footage – linked both to the scene of the crime.

At their trial at the Old Bailey it was suggested that 63-year-old Francis had been 'rubbed out' after reneging on a deal that required him to look after £5 million in Brink's-Mat gold. This has not been confirmed, but his was the ninth death to be linked to this one robbery, and with police admitting they expected more killings as the settling of old scores continued, talk of a Brink's-Mat curse has proved hard to squash.

ROD HALL

The Tabard Centre, Prioress Street, SE1 (2004)

'Stalk-Thin, With the Ears of the Big Friendly Giant'

When police, who had been alerted by friends, arrived to find Rod Hall murdered in his gated, loft-style apartment – stylishly remodelled from two former classrooms in what had been a Victorian school – his death can fairly be said to have sent shockwaves through literary London. While by no means a household name, the 53-year-old was a pioneering and highly successful literary agent whose list of clients included the writers of such well-known films and television series as *The Full Monty*, *Billy Elliot* and *Men Behaving Badly*. He was also credited with creating the first-ever dedicated film and TV tie-in department for a major British publisher, thus playing the role of midwife to a host of other productions such as *Jeeves & Wooster*, *Just William*, *Casualty* and *Babe*.

Tall and skinny – one client described him as looking like an escapee from a Quentin Blake drawing, 'stalk-thin, with the ears of the Big Friendly Giant' – Hall was a popular and well-regarded figure in the publishing world, making his exceptionally brutal killing on 21 May 2004 all the more shocking. His body was discovered by two friends who had called round to his flat, a stylish industrial-chic space with oils by Maurice Cockerill and Terry Frost and bespoke furniture that Hall had treated himself to when *Billy Elliot* received three Academy Award nominations. Inside, the friends found the owner's Siamese cat clearly in great distress, bloody footprints in the shower, and in the second bathroom their friend's blackened and eviscerated corpse lying collapsed in the bath.

Within hours, Hall's business partner in the Rod Hall Agency had pointed police in the direction of a boyfriend, known to colleagues only as Ozzy, providing them with a partial telephone number and the information that he was a student at Newham College.

The clues led directly to Usman Durrani, a 20-year-old part-time security guard from Forest Gate in East London who, it soon became apparent, had stabbed his lover to death. That said, the precise cause of death has never been ascertained because, with between thirty and fifty knife wounds to his body, it had been established that any one of seven different traumas could conceivably have killed Hall.

It is known, however, that the two men had engaged in consensual, if extreme, sex games. The victim had allowed himself to be bound, gagged and suspended over the bath.

After killing him, Durrani took time to clean up before leaving the Tabard Centre and going home to his wife in Beckton. He took with him a camera, on which he had filmed the corpse, an expensive Jaeger-LeCoultre watch and various other personal effects – perhaps in order to make the crime scene look like a robbery rather than a straightforward killing. Shortly afterwards, however, Durrani told a friend what he had done, claiming that he had wanted only to hurt Hall rather than to kill him.

Before long, Durrani was on a flight to Dubai, during the course of which police turned up at his mother's home in Forest

Gate and confirmed that they wanted to interview him in connection with a murder. With hopes evaporating that he had simply been engaged in a robbery that had gone horribly, horribly wrong, the accused was brought back to London and handed over to the police.

He was initially released on bail but then rearrested. Durrani's mood reportedly shifted quickly from bouncy to catatonic in a manner that the interviewing officers found unsettling. It soon became apparent that he was unwell, suffering the effects of what a psychiatrist who examined him for the prosecution called the 'toxic brew' of religion, homosexuality and sadomasochism.

Durrani himself expressed no guilt or regret over what he had done, and at his trial in July 2005 showed very little emotion. He also said very little, except to deny vehemently that he was in any way homosexual and to admit that he was guilty only of manslaughter on what the *Guardian* called 'the grounds that he was mentally ill at the time of the killing'.

He was not judged to be insane, however, even though when he was referred for psychiatric testing it had been agreed that he fulfilled the criteria for a diagnosis of personality disorder. In court, the jury found him guilty of murder. Judge Gerald Gordon ruled that he should serve a minimum term of twelve years and said that he had made Hall 'suffer mentally and physically before his death'.

9

SOUTH-WEST
LONDON

CHARLES BRAVO

The Priory, 225 Bedford Hill, SW12 (1876)

Balham's Black Widow

A large and still-imposing crenelated Gothick fancy, only partially concealed behind blocks of flats, the Priory is one of London's more impressive crime scenes, so it is perhaps appropriate that the evidence of the crime was collected using a genuine silver spoon. The evidence in question was actually vomit, produced by lawyer Charles Bravo, not in court but in bed as he was himself the victim of this celebrated Victorian poisoning.

In December 1875 he had married a young widow, Mrs Florence Ricardo, although it seems that from Bravo's point of view her most attractive attribute might have been the considerable fortune she had inherited on the death of Captain Alexander Ricardo, an alcoholic who had been occasionally inclined towards violence. Briefly the new arrangement had seemed to suit both parties. Florence was able to enjoy the respectability bestowed on her by marriage to a young and thrusting London lawyer, and Bravo could leave his parents' home at No. 2 Palace Green, Kensington now that he could afford a large house of his own with a staff of twelve.

Four months later, however, the latter was suddenly taken violently ill, and two days after that – on 21 April 1876 – Charles Bravo was pronounced dead at the age of 28.

Scooped up on the aforementioned spoon, a pool of vomit aroused suspicion. An autopsy revealed lethal amounts of potassium antimony in Bravo's body. At the time, the compound was a popular emetic, although the quantity indicated that Bravo had almost certainly been poisoned. Suspicion initially fell on his wife, particularly when an examination of her previous husband Captain Ricardo's corpse revealed traces of the same substance.

Florence, however, was by no means the only suspect and it soon became apparent that during the course of his short life Bravo had acquired more than his fair share of enemies. Florence's companion, Jane Cox, was soon in the frame, so too was a neighbour (Florence's erstwhile lover, the hydropathic pioneer, Dr James Gully) as well as a stable hand who was known to have nursed a grudge against the deceased.

Even Bravo himself came under suspicion eventually, with the suggestion from Mrs Fox being that he had administered the emetic himself, either in order to commit suicide or by taking an overdose by mistake. At the inquest the jury refused to consider that the young lawyer had committed suicide, however, and the public certainly preferred the idea that he had been bumped off by his wife or her lover, and that a young woman so keen on respectability was not only a murderer but an adulterer to boot.

Unfortunately, the case was nowhere near as straightforward. As a physician, Dr Gully clearly had the means and possibly the motive, but not the opportunity – and anyway, he had recently ended his relationship with Florence and returned to his wife. Florence certainly had the opportunity to kill her husband but – as far as is known – kept no supplies of the poison at home. And while a conspiracy of the two of them was certainly suggested at the time, it did not prove possible to confirm that any such conspiracy existed.

In the end, a second jury was sworn in and the court was forced to accept that the answer to who killed Charles Bravo that night might never be known. Judge and jury were confident that the victim had had been deliberately poisoned using a lethal dose of a dangerous and well-known emetic, but the assertion was left to stand that 'there is not sufficient proof to affix the guilt upon any person or persons'.

It was an acquittal of sorts, but with the burden of proof traditionally set much lower in the court of public opinion than would be the case in a court of law, both Gully and Mrs Bravo in the end paid a reasonably heavy price. Four years after the court ruling, Florence was herself buried, having apparently drunk herself to death, and, no longer the good doctor, Gully followed her three years later after being ruined both socially and professionally by the controversy surrounding the case.

Precisely what happened will likely always remain a mystery, but for many the finger still points at the widow with two dead husbands who are known beyond doubt to have consumed exactly the same deadly poison.

LEON BERON

Clapham Common, SW4 (1911)

Conspiracy, Cover-Up – or Just Criminal?

Leon Beron was found near Clapham's magnificent bandstand – the largest and oldest survivor of its type in London. He had been battered to death and had a bloody S shape carved into each cheek. Beron was, by most accounts, an unsavoury character: a small-time slum landlord collecting rents on a few rundown properties in Russell Court near St George's in the East. Talk of his death has rarely moved away from rumours of conspiracies and cover-ups at the highest level.

Poorly concealed in sparse undergrowth, the grim discovery on New Year's Day 1911 set the scene for one of London's most controversial murder trials on the run-up to the Great War. Believing the killer to be a strong, left-handed man, it hadn't taken the police long to find their suspect: another Jewish émigré of eastern European origin, Alexander Petropavloff (aka Steinie Morrison), who witnesses recalled seeing lunching with Beron at the Warsaw kosher restaurant at No. 32 Osborn Street, E1.

With recent convictions for house-breaking, Morrison was arrested, initially on the convenient grounds that he had moved home without informing the authorities. He was subsequently charged with the murder after his picture was identified by a cabbie, who claimed to have taken him and a man answering

Beron's description from the East End to Clapham. Another cab driver said he had carried Morrison back to Kennington, while a third, perhaps spurred on by news of a reward being offered by the press, claimed to have driven him back north across the river.

There was also the small matter of a weapon. Morrison had deposited a firearm and a quantity of unused ammunition at the left luggage office of St Mary's – a station on the District Line, located between the present-day stations at Whitechapel and Aldgate East before its closure in 1938 and destruction during the Blitz.

Morrison insisted he had an alibi, claiming to have been at the Shoreditch Empire the previous evening with 16-year-old Janie Brodsky. He said they were there to see Harry Lauder, according to legend the highest-paid performer in the world, and as further corroborating evidence, Brodsky confirmed that the tickets had been bought on the door for 1s apiece.

Unfortunately for Morrison, theatre staff queried this, pointing out that the tickets that night had been 1s 6d, and with Lauder on the bill had been sold out well in advance. The court was also told that Morrison would have been familiar with this particular patch of south London, having worked around Lavender Hill.

The evidence against him was circumstantial but nevertheless looked damning, and with the collapse of his alibi his conviction seemed like a formality. A sentence of death was duly handed down but was almost immediately commuted to life imprisonment by Home Secretary Winston S. Churchill.

In all likelihood, the latter was simply exercising the degree of clemency that his office permitted him, doing so because the judgement looked shaky. The defendant and victim knew each other, having been part of the same East End underworld, but there was never any forensic evidence linking Morrison to the murder, and most of the witnesses were decidedly dodgy themselves and quickly shown to be largely unreliable characters.

Conspiracy theorists had a field day with the case, nevertheless, and continue so to do. For example, when Beron's body was discovered, his wallet was empty: he had clearly been robbed, which could explain the killing. But far more attention has always been paid to his wounds – likened to the f-shaped sound holes on a violin – the suggestion being that the carved 'S' on each cheek prove he was killed by anarchists after being uncovered as a spy.

In particular, these sinister but unsubstantiated charges were used to link Beron's death with the recent Houndsditch Murders and the Sidney Street siege that followed them (see p. 25). Beron, this argument runs, was a police informant who had been killed for leading the authorities to a team of powerful Latvian anarchists who had broken into the Houndsditch jewellers.

The argument did not prove persuasive at the time, however, and perhaps it still fails to do so. Even so, one is still left wondering why one East End villain should go to the trouble of taking another one all the way to Clapham just to finish him off. Morrison certainly continued to protest his innocence but was, nevertheless, to die in prison. Officially, this was put down to his physical state being weakened by repeated hunger strikes, but that has not silenced rumours that he too was bumped off by warders in the pay of someone else.

FREDERICK FIELD

Elmhurst Mansions, SW4 (1936)

A Victim of His Own Vanity

In October 1931, Frederick Field, a general handyman employed to erect 'For Sale' boards for a firm of estate agents, visited the premises of a lock-up at No. 173 Shaftesbury Avenue with his boss. Inside the shop, long since demolished, the two found the body of a 20-year-old streetwalker, Norah Upchurch, who had evidently been strangled a couple of days previously.

Field came under immediate suspicion, having been at the shop two days earlier. When questioned, he produced a confusing account of how he had lent the shop keys to a stranger with a gold tooth: a man dressed in plus fours who claimed to be an electrician. Field even went so far as to identify a man who was being held in custody, only to see him released shortly afterwards when he turned out not to have any gold teeth.

Somewhat surprisingly, Field got away with this and might have continued to do so were it not for his decision in 1933 to seek fame and fortune by selling his story to a newspaper. The newspaper agreed to buy his neatly written confession, in which Field said he had found his victim in Leicester Square, taken her back to the shop, killed her and stolen her handbag. Once published, it ran alongside a much larger story examining the possible ramifications of Berlin's Reichstag fire.

When the story broke, Field was promptly rearrested and charged with murder, but again seemed to have got away with it after withdrawing his confession ahead of the trial. In fact, the newspapers were used to dealing with cranks of this sort who made up stories, and there were a number of inconsistencies in the story once it was read more closely. Most obviously, Field said he had strangled Upchurch with his bare hands, but marks on the skin of her neck indicated that a belt or cord had been used.

Whatever the truth, the judge lost no opportunity in criticising the process of what we know as 'chequebook journalism'. He also felt very strongly that the defendant was a liar and a chancer rather than a murderer, and directed the jury towards a not guilty verdict. Because of this, Field – having dismissed the unfortunate Upchurch as being of 'disreputable class', i.e. beneath his dignity – walked free once again.

By 1936, he was living south of the river in Clapham Manor Street, apparently lying low after deserting from the Royal Air Force station at Hendon, having joined up after losing his job. For this, he was eventually arrested, but not before he had made moves to confess to another murder in order to pick up yet another payment for his story. This time the victim was a middle-aged widow called Beatrice Sutton, whose body had been found in her flat at Elmhurst Mansions on 5 April. She had been strangled and then smothered beneath a pillow.

Fortunately, Field's name still rang a bell in Fleet Street, and he made no real headway before the police began to show some interest in the case. This time – third time around – his luck seemed at last to have deserted him, and on 25 April he was again formally charged with the murder. Admitting in an interview that he did not know the widow and had no ill feeling towards her, he claimed to have 'just murdered her because I wanted to murder someone'.

Once again, he attempted to withdraw this rather bald confession when brought to the dock on 13 May of the same year. Fortunately, on this occasion the judge was not persuaded by his innocence and neither was the jury. According to newspaper reports at the time, it was thought that Field might deliberately have 'put himself on the spot' as he was tired of living but lacked whatever it took to end it all. On 30 June 1936, the authorities made good that shortfall, if indeed it existed, and Frederick Charles Field was hanged at Wandsworth.

In the absence of a reliable confession, it is generally assumed that Field was also responsible for the Shaftesbury Avenue murder, having been crafty enough to insert sufficient inconsistencies into his first newspaper story to ensure that he would not hang for it. In the case of Mrs Sutton, he failed to do this, however, seemingly unable to resist including a wealth of detail which – even once he attempted to deny it – indicated to the prosecution that he knew more than anyone could have about the case based merely on what he had read in the press.

JACOB DICKEY

Baytree Road, SW2 (1923)

'He Wanted Me to Buy a Revolver for Him'

On 11 July 1923, Alexander Campbell 'Scottie' Mason found himself in the dock on a charge of murder, with the prosecution seeking to prove that he was responsible for the death of 39-year-old Jacob Dickey, a taxi driver who had been found dying of gunshot wounds in an undistinguished suburban street running off Brixton's Acre Lane.

Dickey had been driving his fare over from Victoria Station and had turned off Acre Lane into Baytree Road, where he was observed grappling with an unknown assailant. Three shots rang out and, with Dickey collapsing onto the pavement, his attacker made off over a fence into the garden of a property facing onto Acre Lane but now lost beneath a branch of Tesco.

The latter emerged onto the main road through the front door of No. 15, leaving behind a pair of gloves, a flashlight and a distinctive cane or swagger stick with an elaborate gold top and a concealed compartment containing some writing instruments. Without much difficulty, the last object led the CID's Francis Carlin to Eddie Vivian, a known if minor villain sharing digs in Charlwood Street, Pimlico with a prostitute called Hetty Colquhoun.

Vivian quickly implicated his friend 'Scottie', claiming Mason had borrowed the cane while he, Vivian, was ill in bed. According to Vivian, Mason had earlier written to him from prison. 'He wanted me to buy a revolver for him,' police were told, 'and to have it ready to give him when he came to London on getting out.' The two had agreed to do a house-breaking job together, but so far Vivian had done no more than obtain a suitable weapon from a dealer he knew south of the river and hand it to Mason.

Mason was soon pulled in for questioning at Brixton Police Station. Carlin noticed straightaway that his trousers were torn and that he had scrapes on his hands and knees. Just the sort of minor injuries, in other words, that one might sustain clambering into someone else's garden in a hurry.

When he was questioned about the scrapes, 'Scottie' agreed he had got them clambering over a wall but insisted this had been somewhere else, possibly Norbury. Unconvinced by this, Carlin had the two men put into an identity parade, and – after being picked out by the woman through whose garden Dickey's killer had escaped – Mason was sent for trial.

Carlin would probably have liked to nail Vivian too, but Hetty Colquhoun's testimony supported his alibi. Writing his memoirs years later, the detective confirmed that, on reflection, he felt 'Vivian had had no hand in the murder of Jacob Dickey, and I felt equally certain that Mason was the guilty man'.

Once the case got to court, however, and with Vivian as the chief witness for the Crown, Mason and his barrister AC Fox-Davies made strenuous efforts to throw the light onto Vivian, to expose his supposed role in the cabbie's death and, most obviously, to shift the blame from the man in the dock to the one in the witness box.

Vivian was clearly a highly undesirable character; one who was entirely happy to purchase a firearm on behalf of an acquaintance who had been newly released from prison, and who at one point had even suggested that Dickey was a willing participant in the crime. But against this was the evidence which had been built up by Carlin against Mason. (This was, by his own estimation, 'unassailable'.) Vivian, the policeman thought, had nothing to do with the facts of the case against Alexander Mason as proven, and the jury seemed to agree, bringing in their verdict of guilty against him and him alone.

There were, even so, a number of contradictions in the case, and not for the first time the Crown had been forced to rely on the testimony of persons whose reputations would ordinarily have rendered their statements suspect. Because of this, Mason managed to escape the death penalty, and on being granted a reprieve in 1937 he served with honour in the Merchant Navy but did not survive the war.

In the light of this, Carlin wisely kept his own counsel on the decision not to hang him, instead reserving his final words for the victim. Somehow, he wrote later, 'it got about that Jacob Dickey was a straight-up driver, or in other words that he was one of those drivers, of whom there are not a few in the metropolis, who work in connivance with burglars and crooks'. Calling this 'a wicked and outrageous lie', he felt he owed it to the memory of the dead man to make it clear 'that Dickey was an honourable, clean living man' who was murdered, by Mason, while earning an honest pound.

HENDRICK NEIMASZ

HMP Wandsworth, SW18 (1961)

The Last Man to Hang in London

Rather than his crime, it is his punishment which most obviously distinguishes 49-year-old Hendrick Neimasz from London's many other murderers. Convicted of killing two people on 12 May 1961 – Alice and Hubert Buxton, from Brixton – he subsequently entered the history books as the last person to be hanged in the capital ahead of the passing of the Murder (Abolition of Death Penalty) Act in 1965.

His execution took place on 8 September of the same year at Wandsworth. The former Surrey House of Corrections was a place with a fearsome reputation for harshness, based in part, but not solely, on the fact that the warders there were still busily birching and flogging criminals until well into the 1950s.

From 1951 onwards, indeed, it was the only prison in the country permitted to carry out corporal punishment with such implements. Among those who found themselves at the wrong end of the cat-o'-nine-tails were the so-called Mayfair Playboys. This was the gang led by the future 6th Marquess of Bristol, credited with more or less inventing the ram raid when his black Rolls-Royce was implicated in the theft of artefacts belonging to Henry VIII, Elizabeth I and Anne Boleyn from Lord Astor's Hever Castle estate in Kent.

Wandsworth was also the very last prison in Britain to have its own scaffold, the first executions having been held there as long ago as 1878, following the winding down of the Horsemonger Lane Gaol in Southwark. This had required the construction of the charmingly named 'Cold Meat Shed' in a yard, the place where the guilty were to be despatched until 1911 when the gallows were finally moved onto E Wing.

Across the river, Pentonville Prison famously had a collapsible set of gallows in the middle years of the last century and, conveniently situated for King's Cross, St Pancras and Euston stations, these could be shipped by train to wherever they were needed. However, this arrangement was terminated with the passing of the 1965 Act, whereas the Wandsworth scaffold was still being officially checked twice a year to make sure the moving parts were in full working order and was not dismantled until 1994.

Today, sadly, nothing of it remains. Instead, the execution chamber has been converted into a TV lounge for the staff, and a few mementoes such as the trapdoor and hangman's lever have been removed to the Galleries of Justice Museum in faraway Nottingham.

This is perhaps a shame as, in addition to our double murderer, the condemned cell has seen off a number of notorious prisoners over the years. These included William Joyce (better known as Lord Haw-Haw, the Nazi propagandist, who gouged a swastika into his cell wall), the Acid Bath Murderer (see p. 103) and Derek Bentley in 1953. In a case which still generates a lot of ill feeling, the latter was sent to the gallows after the killing of a policeman in Croydon. His accomplice, Christopher Craig, who actually pulled the trigger, was merely jailed as he was under age.

In fact, a good deal of debate surrounds many of the executions at Wandsworth. William Joyce, for example, was technically not guilty of treason since he was a US citizen and not a British one when he took on German nationality and began his broadcasts. Because of this, the historian A.J.P. Taylor argued that in essence he was executed for the very minor offence of making a false statement on a passport; at the same time, many members of the public thought the punishment quite out of proportion for a character widely regarded as something of a joke rather than a serious threat to king and country.

Others among the 135 who met their ends here certainly were traitors, however. Chief among them was John Amery. The Old Harrovian son and brother of Members of Parliament, Amery amassed an impressive seventy-four convictions before joining the fascist side in the Spanish Civil War. In 1941, he was recruited by the Nazis and began making Hitlerite broadcasts from Berlin, his sincere wish being that he could in this way encourage British internees and prisoners of war to fight for Germany.

Towards the end of the war, he switched sides – to support Mussolini – and following his capture by Italian partisans was handed back to the British. After being interviewed by MI5 in November 1945, Amery became the first person to plead guilty to treason in an English court since the Royalist conspirator Summerset Fox in May 1654. His trial was exceptionally short as a result – just eight minutes – and three weeks later, after greeting the hangman Albert Pierrepoint with the words, 'I've always wanted to meet you, though not of course under these circumstances', Amery was dead.

MURIEL MCKAY

20 Arthur Road, SW19 (1969)

'Have a Million by Wednesday Night or We Will Kill Her'

More than forty years after her disappearance, the body of Muriel McKay has never been found. Nor has there been anything to challenge the assumption at the time that she was taken in error by kidnappers who had actually been intending to ransom the wife of media mogul Rupert Murdoch.

Any confusion on this second point is explained by the fact that Muriel was the wife of Alick McKay, Murdoch's deputy chairman at News International. He left for work on 29 December 1969 in Murdoch's blue Rolls-Royce, and returned to Wimbledon that evening to find his neo-Georgian home ransacked and his 55-year-old wife missing.

The telephone had been left off the hook and the little piece of card showing the ex-directory number had been prised from the centre of the rotary dial. His wife's overcoat was missing too, along with a few bits of jewellery. However, kidnapping of this sort was hitherto unknown in this country so, assuming that Mrs McKay had simply left her husband, the police were, to say the least, irritated when McKay called the editor of the *Sun* to get him to run the story of her abduction the following morning.

But within a few hours McKay's suspicions were proved correct when the telephone rang and he was told, 'We are

M3 – the Mafia. We tried to get Rupert Murdoch's wife. We couldn't get her, so we took yours instead. You have a million by Wednesday night or we will kill her.' Having been misled by the appearance in Arthur Road of such a well-known car, the kidnappers made another two dozen calls over the next few weeks, as well as sending a series of increasingly desperate notes from Mrs McKay containing pieces cut from the green woollen suit she had been wearing on the day of her disappearance.

Gradually, a list of instructions was supplied, the first of these requiring Mrs McKay's son to wait in a telephone box on the A10. He was to have a suitcase full of money with him and a telephone call would tell him what to do next. A policeman posing as Ian McKay duly set off carrying a bag containing mostly false banknotes with a layer of real ones on the top.

Following the telephoned instructions, he travelled on to another box at High Cross near Ware in Hertfordshire. There, in an otherwise empty cigarette packet, he found a note telling him where to make the 'drop' and his colleagues settled back to watch who came to collect the money. Unfortunately, after cruising the area for a while, the occupants of a Volvo saloon spotted the plainclothes officers and left the scene.

Another drop was hastily arranged, this time further north towards Bishop's Stortford, where the suitcase was again left under close but covert observation. Once again, a Volvo was seen circling the area but although it left without collecting the money, the police were this time able to get its registration number. Very quickly this led them to Rooks Farm in the village of Stocking Pelham, and to Arthur and Nizam Hosein.

There was no sign of Mrs McKay at the property. However, the two were arrested and charged on a number of different counts after Arthur Hosein's fingerprints were matched to those on the ransom notes.

Hosein, it transpired, was something of a fantasist, and long after his conviction was insisting that a writer who was coming to interview him in a top-security mental hospital must wear a bowtie. Prior to this, when working as a tailor's cutter in Soho, it seems he had conceived a plan to buy some land, live as country gentleman and join the local hunt at Puckeridge.

His scheme was proving expensive, however. Plus, the locals refused to treat him like the gentleman farmer he said he was. Somewhere along the line, he determined that a large injection of cash from Murdoch or an associate would go some way towards solving both problems.

Given all this, it is perhaps hardly surprising that the brothers' defence at the Old Bailey the following September was, like the kidnapping, shambolic and poorly thought out. Neither confessed, but each blamed the other. Arthur further alleged that the whole thing had been masterminded by Murdoch's supposed media rival, Robert Maxwell.

Although the absence of a body might have slightly prolonged the time the jury spent on its deliberations, their guilt was never in much doubt. Arthur Hosein received the maximum sentence of twenty-five years, with an additional fourteen for blackmail and ten for sending threatening letters, and his brother went down for fifteen years. In court, neither revealed what happened to the tragic Mrs McKay.

10

WEST LONDON

WILLIAM WHITELEY

31–57 Westbourne Grove, W2 (1907)

'When Did You Last See Your Father?'

When Edward VII formally opened the City of London's new Central Criminal Court building, a long overdue replacement for the famously pestilential, rat-infested Newgate Gaol, the inscription carved above the main entrance read: 'DEFEND THE CHILDREN OF THE POOR & PUNISH THE WRONGDOER'. The first murder trial at what quickly became known as the Old Bailey, however, involved the child of a millionaire rather than a poor man – one who, while he provided a written confession of his wrongdoing *in advance*, succeeded in escaping the punishment that the court duly handed down.

The man in question was 27-year-old Horace George Rayner. On 24 January 1907, he was charged with shooting dead the self-styled 'Universal Provider' and department store magnate William Whiteley before turning the revolver on himself.

Whiteley claimed to have arrived in London half a century earlier with only £5 to his name, but by this time his eponymous emporium had grown to occupy an entire row of shops on Westbourne Grove. The move to the present site was still four years away, but business in the seventeen departments occupying the row of properties shown here was brisk.

The proud boast was that anything could be obtained in the store, 'from a pin to an elephant', and the January sale was in full swing when a shabbily dressed but formally attired stranger presented himself at the store saying he wished to see the proprietor. The visitor did not have an appointment, but his request was soon granted, and he was shown into Whiteley's office just before lunchtime.

Whiteley lunched punctually at one, so staff were surprised when he appeared at four minutes past and, before returning to his office and closing the door, asked for a policeman to be summoned. Moments later, three shots were heard, and when the police arrived, they found the store owner dead and Rayner lying on the floor with a bullet through his right eye.

A denial of murder was out of the question, for a note in his pocket read, 'To all whom it may concern: William Whiteley is my father, and has brought upon himself and me a double fatality by reason of his own refusal of a request perfectly reasonable. RIP.'

Rayner, it transpired, had told Whiteley that he was his son and he needed help 'in kind or employment'. When Whiteley asked, 'Is that so? And when did you see me last?', he was told it was many years ago, when Rayner was a boy in Kilburn. Afterwards, his mother told him that if he was ever in difficulty he should go and find his 'real father', William Whiteley. With a reputation to protect – as a figure of great rectitude, a self-made Yorkshireman who had succeeded by dint of hard work in making himself rich and secure – the 75-year-old Whiteley had flatly refused to offer any assistance to the young man besides suggesting Rayner flee the country.

In court two months later, Rayner, now sporting a glass eye, claimed not to be able to remember exactly what happened next. He was, however, 'jolly glad' that Whiteley was dead, and it took just minutes for the jury to convict him and for the judge to read out a sentence of death.

The trial had lasted barely five hours, but the case had gripped the nation as stories emerged of a very different William Whiteley to the image he liked to project of the seemingly model employer. Sharp practices and a bullying manner contrasted strongly with his public persona as an obliging, even obsequious, retailer. However, the existence of an illegitimate child surprised few among his workforce, who knew him as a tyrannical lecher who was not above sampling shop girls as if they were simply merchandise on his own shelves.

Back at the Old Bailey, Rayner's written confession had effectively dashed any hope that he might escape the noose on the grounds of 'impulsive insanity', but Edwardian England saw things very differently and rose up. Persuaded by the somewhat sentimental image of a destitute son spurned by a rich father, petitions poured in to the Home Secretary's in-tray – nearly 200,000 signatures were collected in a single week – and bowing to public opinion, Rayner's sentence was soon commuted to life imprisonment.

Rayner himself always insisted he would have preferred to die, and twice attempted suicide before he was eventually released on licence in 1919. As for Whiteley, he perhaps enjoyed the last laugh, leaving well over £1 million behind but with no mention of Rayner or his mother. Instead, the bulk of his estate went towards securing his reputation as a kindly benefactor, with the purchase of a large patch of freehold land near Walton-on-Thames 'as bright, cheerful and healthy spot as possible … and the erection thereon of buildings to be used and occupied as homes for aged poor persons'.

GORDON CUMMINS

187 Sussex Gardens, W2 (1942)
Flat 4, 9–10 Gosfield Street, W1
153 Wardour Street, W1

Six Days, Six Attacks, Four Murders

For a killer or killing spree to really enter the national psyche it always helps if the press can latch onto something memorable, and once Gordon Frederick Cummins was tagged 'the Blackout Ripper', his notoriety was more or less assured. Even so, press coverage of his multiple murders and mutilations was nowhere near as extensive as it would have been in peacetime, as the war had brought shortages of paper and ensured there were plenty of other more newsworthy incidents to be reported. Of course, it also brought the nightly blackouts, designed to thwart the German Luftwaffe, and it was on these that Cummins relied to provide cover for his nocturnal attacks on women he spied out alone after dark.

His first attack, or at least the first for which the 28-year-old RAF serviceman is generally held to be responsible, took place on 9 February 1942 in one of three air-raid shelters that had been opened on Montagu Place. The victim was 40-year-old Evelyn Hamilton, who was described in the press at the time as variously a school teacher and a chemist. He strangled her before stealing her handbag containing £80.

The following day he struck again, another Evelyn, this time Evelyn Oatey. Cummins cornered the Soho prostitute in her flat at No. 153 Wardour Street (a new building on the site now houses offices and an upmarket café) before killing her and slitting her throat with a can opener. From her injuries, police were able to ascertain that the killer was left-handed, as well as picking up a set of fingerprints from the weapon. However, a change in the killer's modus operandi prevented an immediate connection being made with the previous night's attack.

The following night another prostitute was murdered, this time north of Oxford Street at 9–10 Gosfield Street. The victim was 42-year-old Margaret Florence Lowe, who regular punters would have known as 'Pearl'. Found in what is still a small but handsome apartment block, she had been strangled with a silk scarf and then mutilated using a razor, with injuries that the pathologist on the case was later to describe as quite dreadful.

By now, the police began to realise that they had a savage and highly motivated maniac on their hands. This suspicion was to be confirmed just twenty-four hours later with the discovery of Doris Jannouet's body in her flat at No. 187 Sussex Gardens. Once again, she was a prostitute who was known to the police, and again she had been strangled and mutilated.

The following night brought news of no fresh murders, but forty-eight hours after that – St Valentine's Day – Cummins attacked Greta Heywood in a back street off Piccadilly, backing onto the Trocadero where the pair had been for a drink. Heywood made an attempt to fight off her attacker and, after being disturbed by a delivery boy, Cummins took off down Haymarket.

Unfortunately for Cummins, he had dropped the case containing his gas mask, which both service personnel and civilians kept by them during the war. Together with his would-be victim's description, the serial number stencilled on the side of the case – 525987 – led police right to him, albeit not before he had attempted yet another attack on a woman near Paddington Station.

He was quickly traced to his billet in St John's Wood, where, on 16 February, detectives found personal effects belonging to some of his victims. Cummins was questioned about four murders and two attempted murders. Although occasionally representing himself falsely as the illegitimate son of a peer, he had no previous convictions, but the evidence against Cummins was strong, conspicuously so in the case of Evelyn Oatey as his prints matched those found on the tin opener at her flat.

For this reason, and with police resources more than usually stretched in wartime, further enquiries were suspended. The Blackout Ripper was charged with just the one murder and the case was scheduled to be heard at the Old Bailey on 27 April before Mr Justice Asquith. A defence of sorts was mounted but to little avail, and after a trial lasting barely an hour the jury retired to consider their verdict. Returning after thirty-five minutes, they found Gordon Frederick Cummins guilty as charged and he was sentenced to hang.

With a request for an appeal dismissed by the Lord Chief Justice and, according to legend, with at that very moment another air raid over London in progress, the sentence was carried out on 25 June at HMP Wandsworth.

JOHN CHRISTIE

Ornamental garden between Nos 9 and 10 Bartle
Road, W11 (1943–53)

'It Won't Bother You For Long'

Searchers for Hercule Poirot's address will look in vain for
Whitehaven Mansions or Sandhurst Square, and while Sherlock
Holmes enthusiasts will find something at No. 221b Baker
Street, the sad reality is that when Conan Doyle fixed on that
very particular address for his famous detective, the street
numbers petered out at No. 85. Occasionally, things happen the
other way around, however, and genuine addresses can disappear just as quickly as fictional ones seem to spring to life. Of
these, in murder terms at least, the most famous is almost certainly No. 10 Rillington Place, a run-down terraced house in a
small cul-de-sac which was literally wiped off the map after the
truth emerged about the activities of the serial strangler, John
Reginald Halliday Christie.

Today, as a result, few locals seem entirely sure where
Rillington Place was, something which might please their
1950s predecessors, scores of whom were understandably jolly
unhappy with the street's notoriety and thoroughly fed up with
gawkers coming to nose around. After Christie's execution in
1953 for the murder of at least six women, their response was to
petition the local council to do something about it.

Initially, the cul-de-sac, which had been built in the 1860s, was simply renamed Rushton Close after a nearby mews of that name. (Rushton Mews still exists and is frequently mistaken for Rillington Place.) As Rushton Close, it lasted barely twenty years or so, however, as both it and the surrounding area were levelled for redevelopment in the mid-1970s. At that stage, it seems plausible that a decision was taken to deliberately obscure the crime scene still further.

Christie ought perhaps by then to have been old news, but his story had been refreshed in 1961 by Ludovic Kennedy's magisterial book *10 Rillington Place*, and then again ten years later by an excellent film version of it starring Richard Attenborough and John Hurt. Focusing on the wrongful execution of Timothy Evans for Christie's crimes, Kennedy's book was to have far-reaching implications, with the case contributing in large part to the eventual abolition of capital punishment for murder in 1965.

But perhaps it had an effect here too, for a glance at the orientation of Lancaster and Bartle Roads, St Andrew's Square and Wesley Square shows no real commonality or shared boundaries with the former Rillington Place. Instead of following the old layout, the lines of flats and houses south of this stretch of the Circle Line seem very purposely to have been positioned in such a way as to conceal the precise position and location of No. 10. In this, planners avoided any of the new addresses coming to share the same plot or the notoriety of No. 10 Rillington Place. In fact, as near as one can judge, the position of No. 10 is probably now occupied not by a house at all but by the small ornamental garden located between the two addresses shown above.

It is, of course, tempting to wonder how bad a murderer has to be for the scene of his crimes to be completely obliterated in this way, and if Christie's example is anything to go by, the answer seems to be very bad indeed.

Christie was injured by gas in the First World War and briefly became a special constable in the Second World War. He had a history of petty criminal behaviour long before killing his first victim in 1943, a munitions worker and part-time prostitute. Favouring a combination of domestic gas (which at this time was highly toxic), rape while the victim was unconscious and eventual strangulation, Christie's habit was to conceal his victims in the garden and house at No. 10.

In 1948, the bodies of the wife and baby of a fellow tenant, Timothy Evans, were found in an outside wash-house. Both had been strangled, and Christie was called as a witness for the prosecution after the somewhat simple-minded Welshman had confessed to the crime under heavy police questioning. On 9 March 1950, Evans was hanged at Pentonville.

For the next couple of years Christie sensibly bided his time, but in December 1952 he killed his wife and emptied her bank account, managing to explain away her disappearance to anyone who enquired. Then, between January and March of the next year, he despatched three more victims in a similar manner, his activities only coming to light when new tenants in the building peeled away some old wallpaper to reveal a cavity containing three trussed-up bodies.

By now, Christie had quit the property and fled, but on being recognised by a police constable on Putney Bridge he quickly confessed to six murders, and on 15 July 1953 was hanged for one of them, that of his wife Ethel. With his arms pinioned and waiting for the drop, it is said that when he complained that his nose was itching, Albert Pierrepoint was able to assure him, 'it won't bother you for long'.

NEVILLE HEATH

Pembridge Court Hotel, 34 Pembridge Gardens, W2 (1946)

'Put Me Down as Not Guilty, Old Chap'

Affecting the styles and titles of the officer class, but emphatically no gentleman, Neville George Clevely Heath used his good looks and charm to deadly effect as he progressed from deserter through fraudster to sadistic double murderer. The product of an undistinguished private school in Surrey – his father, a barber, had scrimped and saved to find the fees – Heath joined the RAF in 1937 but was soon discharged after going absent without leave from 9 Squadron at Duxford. Thereafter, he spent a similarly brief period in borstal, convicted of a number of charges including obtaining credit by deception and house-breaking.

Following the declaration of war in 1939, Heath joined the Royal Army Service Corps, but his second spell under orders was no more successful, and after giving his guards the slip he fled to Johannesburg and signed on with the South African Air Force. Though gazetted a captain, he was subsequently court-martialled for wearing medals to which he was not entitled and promptly shipped back home to London.

Now in the habit of using a number of different aliases, including 'Group Captain Rupert Brooke' and 'Lieutenant Colonel Armstrong', on 20 June 1946 Heath checked in to No. 34 Pembridge Gardens, which was at this time occupied by the

Pembridge Court Hotel. He signed the register with his own name but appended a suitably impressive-sounding military rank, and was given the key to room No. 4 before leaving to meet a companion, Mrs Margery Gardner, at the Trevor Arms in Knightsbridge.

In theory, Gardner's masochistic tastes should have sat comfortably with Heath's sadistic tendencies, and indeed the previous February the pair had caused some concern at the Strand Palace Hotel when noises coming from a bedroom had prompted the manager to burst in. The 32-year-old film extra refused to make a formal complaint, however, and four months later was evidently perfectly happy to be seen back in Heath's company.

The following afternoon, the two had not yet checked out and at 2 p.m. a chambermaid let herself into the bedroom. Heath was gone and Gardner was dead on the bed with visible bite and whip marks. A post-mortem later revealed ferocious internal injuries, which had been inflicted using a short poker that lay in the fireplace, and her face appeared to have been licked clean of blood.

By now, Heath had left London for the coast and a few days later 'Group Captain Rupert Brooke' checked into Bournemouth's Tollard Royal Hotel – now apartments – where he had dinner with 21-year-old Doreen Marshall. The two had previously met in a neighbouring hotel, and when she was reported missing the following day, Heath helpfully identified her in a police photograph but denied he had any knowledge of where she might be.

Fortunately, at this point one Detective Constable Souter recognised his informant from a picture that had been circulated by Scotland Yard, and asked the group captain whether he was not, in fact, called Heath. This he denied, but a search through his coat pockets revealed a left-luggage ticket leading the officers to a suitcase containing various of his personal effects, including a riding crop that was eventually matched to Gardner's appalling injuries.

Even without the subsequent discovery of Marshall's body, hastily hidden beneath a hedge, it looked like an open-and-shut case. In court on 24 December 1946, the accused was inclined to plead guilty until his brief questioned the wisdom of doing this with a capital crime. 'Alright,' he is reported to have said, 'put me down as not guilty, old chap.'

Really only one question remained to be answered: was Heath sane or insane? When two prison doctors declared him to be sane there seemed to be no escape route left. On 16 October, after requesting a whisky ('better make it a double'), Heath was hanged at Pentonville Prison by Albert Pierrepoint.

In 1980, he enjoyed a kind of second life when he was portrayed by the late Ian Charleson in *The Ladykillers*, and a few years after that he was said to have inspired Nigel Havers' character 'Ralph Gorse' in the television series *The Charmer*.

HARRY ROBERTS

Braybrook Street, W12 (1966)

'I Just Reacted Automatically. I Went on to Autopilot.'

Harry Roberts was a career criminal who started young, selling ration books and black-market goods for his mother. Roberts served time in Gaynes Hall Borstal, which had, a long time previously, been home to Oliver Cromwell and a branch of the wartime SOE. Afterwards, National Service with the army in Malaya taught him the means to kill. When he was demobbed he quickly moved into armed robbery, joining a gang that targeted bookies, banks and offices.

In 1959, he escaped the noose by the narrowest of margins when one of the gang's victims died a year and three days after being attacked. This was two days outside the period that would have seen Roberts charged with murder, and instead he received a seven-year custodial sentence.

The victim on that occasion had been hit hard with a glass decanter, but it was through his subsequent reliance on guns that Roberts gained his reputation as a police killer, before going on to serve one of the longest prison sentences of any British criminal.

On 12 August 1966, a sunny Friday afternoon, Detective Sergeant Christopher Head, Detective Constable David Wombwell and PC Geoffrey Fox were parked in an unremarkable street on the edge of Wormwood Scrubs and on the look-out for car thieves who were known to be operating in the area. The three were sitting in an unmarked police car, unaware that in a van parked a few yards away Roberts and two accomplices were 'tooled up' and discussing the theft of a number of fast cars for use in a robbery they were planning in Northolt.

Their old Standard Vanguard was noticeably decrepit, smoking badly and clearly untaxed, so DS Head and DC Wombwell went over to investigate. As they were searching the van, Roberts, perhaps nervous about what they might find, shot both men with a 9mm Luger, one through the eye and another in the head. Meanwhile, his accomplice, John Duddy, had approached PC Fox who was waiting in the unmarked car and shot him twice at point-blank range. The site is now marked by a small but dignified memorial on the Scrubs side of the road.

According to Roberts himself, what became known as the Massacre of Braybrook Street was 'all over in 30 seconds ... I just reacted automatically. I went on to autopilot.' Nor did it take long for those responsible to be captured, with a tip-off leading police to the second accomplice, Jack Witney, who provided names and addresses for the other two. Duddy was arrested two days later in Glasgow.

Roberts went on the run, before being captured when one of the biggest manhunts in British police history tracked his progress through Epping Forest to a makeshift camp on the Hertfordshire–Essex border.

The triple killing, which the trial judge Mr Justice Glyn-Jones described as 'the most heinous crime to have been committed in this country for a generation or more', had horrified the public and the jury took barely half an hour to find all three men guilty. Execution was no longer possible – the death penalty had been abolished just eight months before what would otherwise have been a straightforward capital crime took place. But Glyn-Jones recommended that the three each serve a minimum of thirty years, telling Roberts he thought it unlikely that any future Home Secretary would 'ever think fit to show mercy by releasing you on licence'.

Duddy was sent to Parkhurst and died in 1981. Amid some controversy, Witney was released on licence five years later, only to meet an appropriately violent end himself when he was bludgeoned to death by an associate with a hammer and an addiction to heroin. Roberts remained inside, however, lending weight to the theory that when Home Secretary James Callaghan promised the 1967 Police Federation Conference, 'because of the abolition of capital punishment some murderers now in prison will die in prison', he may have had Roberts in mind.

In February 2009, however, reports in the press suggested some movement on this and that Roberts was now being actively considered for parole. Unsurprisingly, among those who complained was the Police Federation, whose chairman expressed his horror that such a move was being contemplated for a 'monster [who] has never expressed a word of contrition'. On the contrary, insisted Paul McKeever:

... in prison he developed his artistic skills. He painted pictures showing police officers being killed. He was also well known in the prison community for his baking skills. He baked pies with designs on the crusts that pictured police being killed ... He should stay where he belongs. Decent society does not deserve the displeasure of his company.

As for Prisoner 231191 himself, he told the *Independent* newspaper that after forty-two years banged up, he was no longer Harry Roberts, the police killer, just Harry Roberts, the 73-year-old pensioner. 'Of course I regret what happened and I wish I could turn the clock back, but I can't. It's something that happened in a few seconds but has changed so many people's lives.'

Despite continued protestations, Harry Roberts was released on 11 November 2014 after serving forty-eight years.

OSSIE CLARK

Penzance Street, W11 (1996)

'As Famous as Egg Foo Yong'

Immortalised in a celebrated Hockney double portrait which hangs in Tate Britain and patronised by the likes of The Beatles, Hendrix, Yoko Ono and Twiggy, fifty years ago Raymond 'Ossie' Clark was proof for the young Derek Jarman that decadence was 'the first sign of intelligence'. Unfortunately, Clark's descent into obscurity and poverty was, if anything, to be even more spectacular than his rise to sixties stardom.

In the mid-1960s, Clark had been dubbed the 'King of the King's Road' by the fashion press and considered himself to be 'as famous as egg foo yong'. Meeting the zeitgeist head-on with chiffons, snakeskins and op-art funware described by one commentator as 'sex incarnate', the designer quickly became both a fan and an intimate of rock's aristocracy. But thirty years later, escaping a prison sentence 'by the skin of my teeth' after crashing into a police car and assaulting one of its occupants, he was found stabbed to death in the tiny Notting Hill council flat he had previously shared with his lover – and killer – Diego Cogolato.

His precipitate decline was such that some years earlier, when a *Daily Mail* reader had written in asking, 'Whatever happened to Ossie Clark?', it was left to Clark himself to write in with an answer. Describing his marriage break-up and how he lost his love of fashion, Clark admitted in a letter to the newspaper that he had financial difficulties and had been seeking 'more genuine values' to replace what he called his previous somewhat unreal lifestyle.

Clark ascribed his success to 'my brain and my fingers', but unsurprisingly perhaps, sex and drugs had also played a large part in the designer's rock-and-roll lifestyle. After separating from his wife and business partner, Celia Birtwell, in 1974, the 32-year-old Royal College of Art graduate had then embarked on a series of gay relationships.

By 1987, he was reduced to living partly by barter, producing designs for friends and others in return for free holidays, a sofa to sleep on and, on one occasion, the settling of a bill for the repair of his sewing machine. Living in much reduced circumstances, he finally moved into a tiny council flat in Penzance Street with the Department for Health and Social Security footing the bill.

While he was doubtless something of an oddball in such an environment, Clark is still remembered with warmth and affection by some of his neighbours. His flat was described by one of them as 'organised chaos and artistically neglected'. Clark still allowed himself the odd flight of decadent fancy when this was possible – spare cash would go on multicoloured Sobranie cocktail cigarettes – but he quickly became deflated if anyone raised the subject of his once-stellar career.

Occasionally, it looked as though he might recover some of his early flair. He successfully trained Bella Freud to pattern cut, produced a couple of small collections for the manufacturer Alfred Radley, and would now and again produce one-off designs for close friends. After his death, a neighbour recalled a visit by Bianca Jagger to Penzance Street a few months previously, but such activity was clearly never more than sporadic.

In any event, everything came to a shuddering halt at 6 a.m. on 7 August 1996 when 28-year-old Diego Cogolato dialled 999 and told the operator he thought he might have killed somebody. When police gained access to Clark's flat they found the 54-year-old's body on the floor, his skull smashed and his body bearing the marks of thirty-seven different stab wounds.

In court, Cogolato admitted manslaughter on the grounds of diminished responsibility after what was described as a 'transient psychotic episode' in which he believed his former lover was the devil. He was jailed for six years. It was, said the judge, Mr Justice Douglas Brown, 'a frenzied attack, while you were in a psychotic state which may have been brought on by a combination of drugs, both prescribed and illicit'.

A decade earlier, during one attempted comeback, Clark had been all but ignored by the press, despite catwalk appearances by Marie Helvin and Jerry Hall. But his violent death changed all that, and once again Ossie was front-page news. Prices of his vintage pieces started to climb rapidly and in July 2003 queues formed at the V&A for a retrospective showing his best work. Ossie, posthumously but undeniably, was back on centre stage.

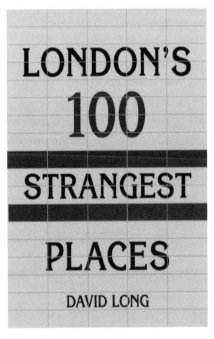

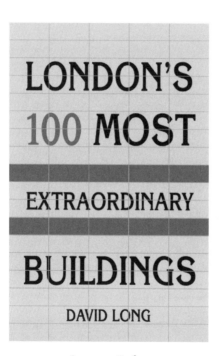

LONDON'S
100 MOST

EXTRAORDINARY

BUILDINGS

DAVID LONG

978 0 7509 8761 5

The History Press
The destination for history
www.thehistorypress.co.uk

Cent
22/09/20